American Naturalization Records
1790-1990

What They Are and
How to Use Them

American Naturalization Records

1790-1990

What They Are and
How to Use Them

by

John J. Newman

Heritage Quest®

North Salt Lake, Utah

Front cover: Certificate of Naturalization of Valenty Nowak, September 21, 1921 (see page 48); Report and Registry of John Christopher Conrad, March 25, 1924 (see page 26); and Certified copy of Declaration of Intention, Court of Common Pleas, City and County of New York, 1852, filed when James Lyons petitioned for citizenship in Carroll County, Indiana.

Heritage Quest, a division of SierraHome®, PO Box 540670, North Salt Lake, UT 84054-0670
Published 1985 by Indiana Historical Society. Second Edition 1998 by Heritage Quest
Printed in the United States of America
03 02 01   7 6 5

Library of Congress Catalog Card Number: 98-71939
ISBN: 1-877677-91-4

 **Contents**

List of Illustrations vii

Research Strategies 1

Alien Residents and Undocumented Citizens 7

Naturalization Courts 9

Naturalization Laws 1790 - 1906 13

Naturalization Laws 1906 - 1990 17

Naturalization Case Law 21

Unique 19th Century Procedures 23
    Registry 23
    Naturalization Investigations 24

Types of Records 33
    Summary 47

Derivative Citizenship 53

Citizenship Based on Military Service 57
    Veterans' Naturalization Procedures 57
    World War I Alien Registration 58

Special Naturalization Actions 65
    Land Purchase 65
    Native-born Naturalized Women 66

Accessing the Records 67
    Work Projects Administration Naturalization Project 67
    Centralization of Naturalization Records 68

Research Procedures 69

Pointers 77

Contents

Appendix I: Naturalization Processes by Person and Time 79
Appendix II: Census Records—Questions Relating to Foreign-born and Citizenship ... 89
    State Census Records 99
Appendix III: Internet Connections for Naturalization Research 101
Appendix IV: Definition of Select Terms 103
Appendix V: Naturalization Inventory Checklist 107
    Naturalization Inventory 110
    Cross References 111
Notes 113
Bibliographical Essay 123
    Sources on Naturalization 123
    General Publications 125
    Sources of Records 126

 # Illustrations

I. OLD LAW NATURALIZATION FORMS

Old Law Declaration of Intention .... Illus. 1 25

Registry and Declaration .... Illus. 2 26

Registry and Declaration of Intention .... Illus. 3 27

Post Registry Period Declaration of Intention .... Illus. 4 28

Notice of Intention .... Illus. 5 30

Declaration of Intention Showing Error in Name .... Illus. 6 31

Certified Copy of Declaration From Burned County .... Illus. 7 34

"Final Oath" .... Illus. 8 36

Minor's Petition .... Illus. 20 54

Naturalization Record from Court Order Book .... Illus. 24 71

II. POST SEPTEMBER 1906 NATURALIZATION FORMS

Declaration of Intention

   Certificate of Arrival .... Illus. 9 37

   Form 2214, Facts for Petition for Naturalization .... Illus. 10 38

   Form 2202, Declaration of Intention .... Illus. 11 41

   Form 2202 L-A, Declaration of Intention .... Illus. 12 42

   Biographic Information Form .... Illus. 13 43

   Declaration of Intention of David Duell .... Illus. 18 51

   Voter Registration Form .... Illus. 19 52

Petition

   Form 2204, Petition for Naturalization .... Illus. 14 44

   Form 2204 L-A, Petition for Naturalization .... Illus. 15 46

Certificate

    Certificate of Naturalization .... Illus. 16 48

    Stub of Certificate of Naturalization .... Illus. 17 49

III. WORLD WAR I DRAFT REGISTRATION CARDS

    WWI Registration Card, First Call .... Illus. 21 61

    WWI Registration Card, Second Call .... Illus. 22 62

    WWI Registration Card, Third Call .... Illus. 23 63

IV. CENSUS AND STATISTICAL REPORTS

    Table 1   Immigration to the United States, 1820 - 1956 92

    Table 2   Foreign-born Population, by Country of Birth, 1890 - 1910 93

    Table 3   Length of Residence in the United States 94

    Table 4   Year of Immigration by States & Regions 95

    Table 5   Foreign-born White Males 21 Years and Over, Naturalized 96

    Table 6   Foreign-born White Population by Citizenship and Country of Birth 97

    Table 7   Naturalization Statistics, 1907 - 1947 98

# Research Strategies

"The Congress shall have power . . . to establish a uniform rule of naturalization."
(U.S. Constitution, Article I, Section 8)

Find the record to find the relative.

Genealogy can be simple. The family historian seeks the following information: name, date, place, event, and relationship. To gain this data, he or she uses three classes of records: descriptive, locator, and identifier. Finally, such information from records is reviewed for accuracy and completeness. But why are so many unsuccessful in their quest? "Genealogy," the dictionary states, is "the study or investigation of ancestry and family histories."[1] Yet, too many family historians concentrate on the ancestor and not on the "study" or "investigation." The successful genealogist concentrates on *records* and develops a "genealogy of records" containing information helpful in providing ancestral names, dates, places, events, and family relationships.

American Naturalization Records, 1790 -1990, is a genealogy of the citizenship process. It provides fine detail on naturalization procedures. This is necessary to furnish information helpful in locating an ancestor's naturalization record. As a records genealogy, this publication will *name* typical courts, authorized or unauthorized, that naturalized. By researching the history of courts in a particular county, one might find that three or more courts natu-

How to Use This Book

This study is not a history of naturalization laws and procedures; it abstracts record requirements and processes from such laws and rules and compresses over 200 years of legislation and tradition into a few pages. At first blush, this may seem to be overwhelming. The reader must expand the appropriate section describing those naturalization requirements which relate to the time period of the ancestor. Know as much about your immigrant's life as possible to place him or her in a specific time, locality, and neighborhood. What could have motivated citizenship--the need to own land, to vote, peer pressure? What local traditions and unusual conditions affected the naturalization process? The degree of successfully locating citizenship records increases by abstracting from this work, those legal requirements and appropriate forms which apply to your research, and by developing an understanding of which courts could and did naturalize during the immigrant ancestor's lifetime. Divide, expand, and conquer!

ralized aliens concurrently. *When* the process occurred is critical, since specific laws, at different times, required different records, varied procedures, or applied to special classes of aliens. Determining *where* a naturalization occurred is most frustrating since a declaration of intention might have been issued in a county unknown to the family historian, or worse, where court records have been burned, and the petition occurred elsewhere. Upon understanding the distinct naturalization procedures, along with knowledge of how courts filed and recorded their proceedings, the likelihood of success increases immensely. One is never certain that an immigrant ancestor was naturalized. If so, where, when, and what records survive? This "genealogy of the naturalization process" is designed to help.

Perhaps nowhere else is knowledge about records throughout time of greater value than when one seeks naturalization information. For most citizen forbearers, events such as birth, marriage, and death are core research objectives and usually are simple to acquire. But to connect an ancestor to the Old World from the New is not so easy. The researcher must remember that naturalization always has been a *voluntary* action. While land ownership, voting, or monetary benefits strongly influenced individuals, probably a majority of foreign-born residents never opted for citizenship.

The first objective, then, is to seek information to determine if an alien ancestor was ever naturalized. If so, what process was in place during his or her life? Second, what types of naturalization records exist? To locate a naturalization document, the genealogist must know as much as possible about the "life-cycle" events of an ancestor: vital statistical data, residences, and time periods. He or she must connect these events to identifier records such as census, death, voting, military, and land records. He or she must seek birth and Bible records, school registers, military records, marriage and divorce documents, publications reflecting an individual's participation in politics, fraternal and social organizations, deeds and mortgages, and death and burial registers.[2] Finally, the genealogist must understand naturalization procedures and records.

To assist the researcher develop a strategy, records can be classified into three major categories: descriptive, locator, and identifier. *Descriptive records* put a person in a time and place. These include histories, maps, migration studies, "how-to" books, and research about record types, such as this publication. One frequently arrives at a point where further progress is stopped. But, if one studies land ownership maps to determine who that ancestor's neighbors were, for example, research on those neighbors might provide a necessary clue. Individuals do not live or die in isolation. They interacted, witnessed the deeds and marriages of neighbors, intermarried, and frequently migrated together from place to place. For example, in 1837 two German land speculators living in Cincinnati laid out a settlement in Indiana called Oldenburgh, for immigrants from Germany. Since that land quickly sold out, they repeated the process in Teutopolis, Illinois, and in Clayton County, Iowa. The appropriate church histories provide the necessary link.

Locator records direct the genealogist to lists of names and to records of genealogical value. They, too, link a name to a date and a place. Helpful are state gazetteers and occupational, city[3] and county directories, and especially indexes. Of greatest value are those locator records that cover extensive periods of time and geographical regions. Indexes to federal land patent and homestead records, to deeds, to censuses, and to the variety of regional, state, and local indexes to naturalization records, are most helpful. The user must realize that these finding aids are the result of another's interpretation of the spelling of a name as well as the potential that a name was missed. Illus. 4 shows the declaration of intention of Philip Hyde, who arrived at New York City June 2, 1830. His name is not indexed in the appropriate ship passenger list but does appear on the manifest. Since indexes are quite valuable, the following may be helpful:

In the ideal world, an index performs two functions:

> (1) it tells one **if** a person or information exists in the record; and if so

> (2) it tells one **where** that person or information can be found within the record.

In the real world, indexing is as good as the indexer, and few standards have existed until recently. When events cannot be classified easily, as those relating to only one party in the judicial naturalization process, deficiencies may appear. Indices serve as locator records. Understanding the judicial process is key to understanding the completeness of its index.

There are a number of indexing systems in use in courthouses:

> (1) surname;

> (2) family name;

> (3) given name; and

> (4) guide letter.

The most common is the surname index. Under each letter of the alphabet, in order of entry, is the surname of the party. The division may be for 12, 24, or 26 letters. In larger counties, or for general indices covering many records over long time periods, the other three index systems have been used. Of these, indexing under the family name is the least used in Indiana but is common in Kentucky. Somewhat popular is the given name index. It requires that one know the initial of the given name to locate the index data. The surname is repeated for each different given name. Finally, there is the guide letter index system, such as the Russell System, popular in Western Pennsylvania.

There are two problems using indices. First is the spelling of the name. For instance, the Eads name has been spelled at least twelve different ways; and in one census, a Mr. Jeter was listed under Geeter. This difficulty is especially true where a large influx of Germans settled in a region where clerks were English. One frequently sees their misspelling of names on naturalization records. Before searching for a name in court records, write your ancestor's name phonetically with as many spelling variations as possible. A helpful guide is a list of about 5700 surnames, with variations, from the 1790 census, which appeared in *A Century of Population Growth*, U.S. Census Bureau, 1909.[4] While most names then were of English origin, and the greatest misspelling of names in the nineteenth century usually were German, the following example can suggest how one can search for a name under variant spellings: Haun=Haan, Hahn, Han, Hans, Hawn, Hohn, Holme, Honn, Hons. For determining alternative spellings in the twentieth century, city directories include name variations.

Second, *where* the clerk placed the index entry in the record when only one party was involved, as with a naturalization, can be equally frustrating. Check the index under the following as well as under the name.

I = IN RE

E = EX PARTE

M = MISCELLANEOUS

N = NATURALIZATION

O = ORDER

P = PETITION

Index systems change over time. If the name is not indexed under any of the above, then examine each index page. One can only guess how an English clerk deciphered the first letter of a German surname. One clerk recorded each ex parte proceeding under "F" for "folio entry."

The last class of records are *identifier records*, which distinguish an individual from all others. Identifier records link names to events and help prove relationships. An important distinction is that identifier information comes *from* records while locator data describes information *about* records or individuals, subject to another's interpretation. Birth, marriage, divorce, death records, census enumerations, church registers, land records, and court records, especially estate and probate proceedings, are examples of identifier records. These are the records one seeks because identifier records are original and usually contemporary with the event. They are created by or under the direction of the participating ancestor. But to use these types to best advantage, the family historian must understand the conditions under which such records were created. For naturalization documents, one must understand the laws, the legal process, and the problems associated with locating and using them fully.

Finally, to gain success in locating naturalization records, the family historian must know the nature of court record keeping systems, especially before September 1906, when federal forms and procedures dictated a uniform structure. An individual filed a document, called a pleading, as a declaration of intention, with the clerk of court. The document, along with any others that came forth, such as affidavits, was *filed*, as a case or cause, which was added to all other cases scheduled before the court. The judge acted upon the pleading or case, and his decision was *recorded* in the official journal of that court. If the court handled many types of cases, the judge's decision could be placed in one of several separate record minute or order books, as civil, probate, or chancery ledgers. Sometimes the volume of citizenship records was so large that the judge's decisions were entered into separate naturalization ledgers. Upon disposal of the naturalization case, the pleadings, frequently called "loose papers," were stored, usually quarter-folded, in pull drawers with all other cases disposed on a particular day. Ledger books contained the decisions of the judge. It is important, then, that the researcher locate both the *original papers*, as *filed*, as well as entries in the books, since the latter probably does not contain all the information found in the original papers.

This publication suggests ways to incorporate descriptive records about one's relatives with locator records. Once the genealogist achieves this, he or she can then study the laws, the record creating and keeping processes, and the records themselves. The final element of this strategy is a suggested methodology to locate naturalization records that identify the immigrant ancestor. This publication is not a list, nor is it an inventory of locations of naturalization records. It provides knowledge helpful in determining decisions a forbearer may have made regarding citizenship and more importantly furnishes an understanding of the value of the naturalization process in family history.

The quality of information varies greatly for the three broad periods of naturalization record keeping, 1790 - 1850's, 1850's - 1906, and after 1906. The first two periods have been the most frustrating. The degree of completeness, lack of detail, and errors in record keeping are modern concerns concisely commented upon by Richard D. Campbell, Commissioner of Naturalization, remarking on the need for federal supervision of admission of resident aliens to citizenship, which came about as a result of the far-reaching naturalization act of June 29, 1906, effective the following September 27th: "To those who will take the trouble to compare the chaotic and disorderly conditions which characterized the procedure for more than a century of our national existence with the dignity, uniformity, and regularity of the present system, it must appear to be a matter of inexplicable carelessness that the reform should so long have been delayed."[5]

Many authors have discussed naturalization records in searching for an ancestor and have described their nature and location. Consult these books and articles.[6] But in pursuit of the genealogist's quest to know how ancestors were naturalized; when, where, and what records exist; what information is given; and how to proceed, this different research approach has equal value.

This publication will review the "dignity, uniformity, and regularity" of the American naturalization system from its beginning as a federal process. Throughout its history, what procedures were

The reader will note many illustrations and examples from Indiana sources. This is not to suggest that this is a book on Indiana naturalization records, but only that the author understands the structure, unique record systems, and details for Indiana. While about 80% of record keeping throughout the United States is similar, knowledge about the other 20% must be ascertained on a state-by-state and county-by-county basis. The aim is to share the fact that by being aware of unique details on record keeping, a greater chance of locating all records is possible. These Indiana illustrations serve as a model to help one understand each state's naturalization procedures (in as much detail as possible). Both archivists and this book can suggest means for the researcher to achieve the same level of understanding for any state or county as this author has for Indiana records.

required to generate what records? What information would one expect to find? What facts generally are not known, and what are the reasons why anticipated data may not exist? This study will discuss a general functional history of naturalization, the steps leading to citizenship, special legislation and factors affecting who could be naturalized, and the records resulting from these laws and procedures. It is based upon the author's understanding of naturalization laws and procedures to aid the user of this book find naturalization links.

Government records are not created for genealogical purposes but document some legal or administrative function, like providing a service, regulating, or taxing. Thus, to explore naturalization records for genealogical value, one must study this process in its bureaucratic environment.

Alien Residents and Undocumented Citizens

Not all alien residents were naturalized. In 1830, 108,000 unnaturalized foreigners represented one percent of the nation's ten and a half million people.[7] The 1890 through 1930 censuses questioned foreign-born whites on their immigration and citizenship. These census fields with appropriate directions are given in Appendix II. For this period, those who were not naturalized or whose citizenship status was unknown represented 28.7 percent, on the average, of all those of foreign births:[8]

census	foreign-born	number	% nat'l	% dec	% alien	% unk
1890	all males, 21 +	4,348,459	58.5	05.4	27.4	08.4
1900	white males, 21+	4,904,270	58.0	08.4	18.7	14.9
1910	white males, 21+	6,548,934	46.2	08.7	33.6	11.5
1920	white males, all ages	7,269,191	47.3	15.6	32.0	05.2
1920	white females, all ages	5,986,203	50.5	01.4	41.5	06.6
1930	white males, all ages	7,153,709	60.6	13.2	23.1	03.2
1930	white females, all ages	6,212,698	56.8	04.9	34.4	03.9

The 1914 report of the Bureau of Naturalization noted, "There are now in this country probably some millions of Unnaturalized aliens and probably more than a half million of valid but unused declarations of intention."[9] Theodore H. Harris, a Louisville, Kentucky, photographer who arrived in Philadelphia from Nova Scotia via Brazil in 1844 and who, after a successful career behind the camera, became a banker and died a millionaire in 1909, never was naturalized. Many aliens lived their lives as positive contributors to their community and new nation without formally acquiring citizenship. Some states' constitutions permitted aliens who filed declarations of intention the franchise;

and, except for certain periods when the naturalization process was required, ownership of land was not conditioned upon citizenship. Many thought they were citizens by derivation from parent or spouse, while others found lack of citizenship no impediment to living their private lives.

In addition to individuals not exercising their desire for citizenship, legislation or treaties granted citizenship to people living in whole territories. Residents of the United States, when the Constitution was adopted in 1789, automatically became citizens, as did those living in territories annexed to the United States. Thus, when territory was added, as the Louisiana Purchase, 1803, Florida, 1819, the Republic of Texas, 1845, the Oregon Territory, 1846, the cession of the Mexican Territory, including California, 1848, and the Gadsden Purchase, 1854, residents of these regions automatically became citizens. Sometimes special congressional acts were passed. An act of May 18, 1872, gave blanket citizenship to those born in the territory of Oregon, who were subject to the jurisdiction of the United States on May 18, 1872. An act of April 30, 1900, granted citizenship to residents in the territory of Hawaii, as did an act of March 2, 1917, to those living in Puerto Rico. All Danish citizens, natives living in the Virgin Islands on January 17, 1917, and those born there after that date, were deemed citizens under an act of February 25, 1927.

Those who could exercise naturalization rights represents the final category. From the first act of Congress, 1790, forward, naturalization language has been gender-neutral. These acts, through the 1820's, permitted "any alien, being a free white person," to become a citizen. These early laws granted "children of such person so naturalized, under the age of twenty-one" citizenship on the strength of the naturalization of that person. Section 2 of the 1802 act requiring registry, referred to "he and she." The Act of 1855, granting citizenship to women who married, affected any woman "who might herself be lawfully naturalized." While these laws permitted any woman to become a citizen on her own, from 1790 forward, few apparently did.

Race was eliminated under an act of April 9, 1866,[10] and by the Fourteenth Amendment to the Constitution, proclaimed July 28, 1868. The Act of 1906 applied to "any alien," with no reference to race. Aliens from certain counties, as the Chinese, however, were denied citizenship under the Act of May 6, 1882. It, as amended, was repealed by the Act of December 17, 1943. Native American Indians were granted citizenship under the Act of June 4, 1924. However, under the Act of November 6, 1919, honorably discharged Indians who served in World War I could, "upon proof of such discharge and after proper identification before a court of competent jurisdiction, and without other examination, . . . be granted full citizenship." The Act of June 24, 1935, permitted citizenship for honorably discharged Chinese who served in World War I.

Naturalization Courts

Naturalization has been the judicial procedure flowing from Congressional legislation in fulfilling its Constitutional power. "While there had been various Federal naturalization laws, beginning with the year 1790, they had enumerated general controlling principles only. The proceeding was a judicial one . . . . Nor was there any provision made for the supervision of the subject by any Federal administrative agency, until the basic naturalization Law of 1906."[11] For the nineteenth century, the emphasis was on naturalization; for the twentieth, equal importance was given to uniformity of implementation. Naturalization laws reflect two distinct approaches institutions take that affect record keeping. The legislative body can either assign a *function* by statute to be performed by designated governmental offices; or it can create a single administrative *structure,* a bureaucracy, to perform and supervise such a function. The resulting records and their value for genealogy differ greatly.

Congress in 1790, 1795, and 1802, required naturalization to occur in a court of record, that is, one having common law jurisdiction, and a seal and clerk or prothonotary."[12] The 1906, 1940, and 1952 acts continued this practice, permitting any court to naturalize, having a seal, a clerk, and jurisdiction in action at law or equity, or law and equity, in which the amount in controversy is unlimited."[13] These courts have had a variety of names, varying from state to state, as supreme, circuit, district, common pleas, chancery, probate, superior, and equity.

The courts and their clerks perform the following operations relating to records: they file, record, and generate proceedings. In the nineteenth century, depending on the state, court, judge, and clerk, these functions were performed with little consistency. Sometimes declarations of intention only were filed, that is, kept and added to the paper storage of the office. By the early 1850's most courts were also recording these in ledgers, such uniformity only being controlled by the style of ledger sold by the vendor.[14] However, the entire purpose of having a court of record was to generate a permanent record of its proceedings, so until September 27, 1906, an entry of the court order of naturalization *had to be* enrolled in the court's official record, be it called a minute or order book.[15]

Naturalization jurisdiction, or the power of the judge to hear naturalization cases within a defined geographical area, was not exclusive to one court, however. Congressional statutes stated that jurisdiction extended only to alien residents within the judicial districts of such courts. Jurisdiction of federal, district, and circuit courts[16] could be state-wide as well as could that of state Supreme Courts.[17] The Indiana State Supreme Court naturalized from 1856 to 1906; the Minnesota Supreme Court, 1858 - 1910; and the Nebraska Supreme Court, 1870 - 1901.[18] Apparently the Supreme Courts of Idaho, Iowa, Maine, New Jersey, South Dakota, and others did likewise. On the county level, courts may have been created to exercise specific jurisdictions, such as civil, probate, equity, or criminal proceedings. Different courts, in a single county, also could naturalize concurrently with entries made in separate ledgers. A single court may have adjudicated several different types of cases with proceedings recorded in separate probate minute books, chancery decree books, or civil order books; and a clerk could have entered a naturalization proceeding in any one. Search each of these official proceedings, created in the nineteenth century, for the court order of naturalization, especially when jurisdictions overlapped.

What is a court of record, then? It is one whose proceedings were enrolled as a perpetual memorial; it had common law jurisdiction, a seal, and a clerk. All four elements were necessary for a court to confer citizenship.[19] The 1906 law narrowed jurisdiction to courts exercising unlimited civil jurisdiction, adding that the amount in controversy had to be unlimited.

Various citizenship records of the nineteenth century show that more courts were naturalizing than should. The 1905 *Report to the President of the Commission on Naturalization* stated that 5,160 courts (157 federal and 5,003 state and territorial) could or had been exercising naturalization jurisdiction.[20] A 1903 investigation for the Attorney General found many courts illegally exercising naturalization jurisdiction.

> Among these usurping courts are the police courts of Maine, New Hampshire, Vermont, and Kentucky; criminal courts and municipal courts of limited jurisdiction strictly defined by statute, and probate courts of various States, including New York, Ohio, Illinois, Wisconsin, South Dakota, and Kentucky. In Ohio the probate court has been acting in each of the 88 counties of the State since 1841, and the total number of certificates issuing out of those courts reaches an aggregate of over 100,000. I find, also, that the Territorial probate court of the Territory of Utah also issued hundreds of certificates.[21]

Acts of Congress validated the naturalization proceedings and records of some of these courts: Criminal Court, Cook County, Illinois (June 29, 1906); Territory of Hawaii (May 27, 1910); City (Police) Court, Louisville, Kentucky (August 24, 1912); County Court, Davidson County, Tennessee (June 23, 1913); and in the State of Montana (August 11, 1916).

After the 1906 act took effect, however, fewer courts were naturalizing than were needed. From that date through 1910 no federal court in Iowa naturalized. For 1907 and 1908 the same was true for federal courts in Kansas, and likewise in 1907 for Vermont. For two years no naturalization occurred in state courts in Rhode Island.[22] A variety of regulations and lack of fees influenced these actions.

> In most of the States, especially in the West, the bulk of the business of naturalization has been confined to the State Courts, as in Ohio, Michigan, Minnesota, Wisconsin, Montana, Nebraska, North and South Dakota, Oregon, Texas, Utah, Washington, California, Idaho, Indiana, Iowa, and Kansas. This is also true of a few of the Eastern States, such as Connecticut, Maryland, New Hampshire, and New Jersey. In those States, however, in which the great bulk of the naturalization is conferred (New York, Pennsylvania, and Massachusetts) the Federal courts are chiefly resorted to.[23]

By studying state-by-state statistics that appear in the annual reports of the Bureau of Naturalization through 1920, one can create a strategy for what courts had greater potential for naturalization.

One should be prepared to interpret the concept of "court of record" loosely. Indiana created a Board of County Commissioners as an administrative body for each county with certain judicial-like powers. It had a clerk, a seal, and a permanent record of its proceedings. The Greene County, Indiana, county commissioners took their judicial powers to heart; and at their June, 1842, meeting, they received the petition for citizenship of Robert Tibitts and entered an order for naturalization in their record book. There is no corresponding judicial court order in the county's circuit or probate courts.[24]

Starting in 1908 the U.S. Department of Labor began issuing *A Directory of Courts Having Jurisdiction in Naturalization Proceedings*. This listed courts by counties alphabetically by state, with the first state entries for federal courts. In 1908, 2,244 courts naturalized. By 1932, 3,844 courts potentially had the jurisdiction.[25] The 1963 directory, issued by the Department of Justice, is especially helpful. It lists the courts as "active," "inactive by local agreement," "relinquished jurisdiction," or "never active." If a court no longer naturalized, the directory told what court assumed its jurisdiction.[26] If a court relinquished its jurisdiction, another trial court in the county may have naturalized or else defaulted to a federal court. Also, some states may have had courts separate from the county seat, as in Indiana and Kentucky. Lake County, Indiana Superior Courts in East Chicago, Gary, and Hammond naturalized as well as the courts in the county seat of Crown Point.

There are six methods of becoming a citizen of the United States:[27]
   1) By birth in the United States;
   2) By naturalization in a court exercising naturalization jurisdiction, through October 1, 1990;
   3) By derivation through the naturalization of one's parent(s) or from 1855-1922 by marriage to the petitioner;
   4) By acquisition at birth through citizen parent(s) if born abroad, as in military service;
   5) By legislation collectively naturalizing certain groups of persons;
   6) By annexation of territory to the United States.

The naturalization process required five distinct procedures:

1) Report and Registry of Aliens, 1798-1828, separate from or combined with

2) Declaration of Intention;

3) Petition for Naturalization;

4) Order of court granting citizenship, based upon the petition and oath of allegiance;

5) Certificate of Naturalization (given to person being naturalized).

Registry did not always occur at the same time or in the same court as did the filing of the declaration. The descriptive contents of the declaration varied extensively. Some courts created ledgers for "final papers" or granted petitions. Until 1906, and sometimes thereafter, the court's order always was recorded in its proceedings, this being the purpose of conferring naturalization in a court of record, to create a permanent memorial of an alien's citizenship. After this process was complete, a certificate was issued to the petitioner. To be successful, researchers must understand each step and the information required and search until they find documentation of each procedure.

Naturalization Laws
1790 - 1906

The first federal naturalization law, March 26, 1790, probably was based upon the 1779 statute of Virginia, one of seven former colonies having state naturalization laws, 1776-1789. This 1790 act required a two-year residence in the United States and one year in the state. The individual had to be of good character and was required to make an oath to support the Constitution. His or her application could be filed in any common law court of record. No declaration of intention was required.

The first act was repealed and replaced by an act of January 29, 1795, which required a declaration of intention to be filed three years before admission as a citizen, residence of five years in the United States and one in the state where naturalized, an oath of allegiance, good moral character, renunciation of any title of nobility, and of allegiance and fidelity to the reigning foreign sovereign. This, with slight modification, became the cornerstone of all future naturalization proceedings.

However, the 1795 act was supplemented and amended by the most stringent naturalization law, the Act of June 18, 1798. It increased the requirement for citizenship. For example, an alien needed fourteen years' residence in this country. It also required clerks of courts to forward copies of declarations of intention, the report of registry, and naturalization proceedings to the United States Secretary of State.[28]

This law was repealed by the Act of April 14, 1802, which reenacted the basic provisions of the 1795 act and 1798 registry requirement. This statute, while amended and added to, became the naturalization code of the nineteenth century.

The first of these changes, passed March 26, 1804, permitted naturalization of aliens residing in the United States between June 18, 1798, and April 14, 1802, without previous declaration of intention. An act of March 3, 1813, required the alien's residence to be continuous. An act of March 22, 1816, reinforced the language of the 1802 code that both the registry and declaration had to be exhibited on the application for citizenship if the applicant arrived after June 18, 1812. The Act of

May 26, 1824, validated naturalization certificates which did not comply with the 1816 act. This registry requirement was repealed by an act of May 24, 1828. The 1824 act also reduced the time between filing a declaration and naturalization from three years to two. The last major general amendment was the 1828 act which also stated that any alien residing in the United States between April 14, 1802, and June 18, 1812, who had continued his or her residence might be admitted to citizenship without having made a previous declaration of intention.

These general laws also had special features for wives, widows, and children, which are discussed under derivative citizenship. Later laws, with the exception of an act of June 26, 1848, which repealed the last clause of section 12 of the March 3, 1813 law, dealt with derivative citizenship or naturalization of veterans, also addressed later. One special case was the declaration of intention. Naturalization acts of 1795 and 1802 required that an alien shall have declared before the proper *court* his or her intention to become a citizen. Most aliens filed this declaration with the *clerk* of court rather than with the court itself. The Act of May 26, 1824, validated past declarations made before the clerk and not the court. The Act of February 1, 1876, amended the 1802 law to permit declarations to be filed with the clerk. The 1906 and later acts carried forward this provision.

In addition to federal statutes, California, Connecticut, Maine, Maryland, Massachusetts, New Hampshire, New Jersey, New York, Ohio, Pennsylvania, Rhode Island, Vermont, and Washington passed laws regarding naturalization in state courts. Massachusetts, New Jersey, and New York required a copy of the naturalization record be forwarded yearly by February 1 to the Secretary of State. The laws affecting Baltimore, Maryland, and Rhode Island required publishing the petition for naturalization in some local paper. The Maryland act stated, " . . . such notice shall state the name, place and date of birth of the applicant, the time of his arrival in this country, the place at which he arrived, and the place or places of residence of the petitioner since his arrival, and the names of his witnesses."[29] The 1903 Rhode Island law was less specific.

The Act of March 3, 1903, prohibiting anarchists from citizenship, represents the problems and frustrations of implementing law by policy and not procedure. The Act provided that, to validate a judicial order of naturalization, a court's proceedings had to show that the applicant had complied with the 1903 and other naturalization acts and that an oath had been administered stating the applicant was not an anarchist. Also, affidavits of witnesses had to be recorded, or the certificate of naturalization was void. An investigation of the implementation of this law concluded that thousands of certificates were invalid. The report observed:

> In some courts, under the law of March 3, 1903, the affidavits of the applicant and his witnesses are entered in full in separate naturalization books of record printed in duplication of the affidavits; in other courts the affidavits are filed and afterwards bound in book form, and are the only record made.

As a result of the matter being left to the various judges and clerks there have been prepared and are now being used the greatest variety of affidavits and certificates ever devised under a single law, some of the certificates containing less than 200 words and others 4,000 words.[30]

Many courts, not aware of the 1903 law, continued to issue certificates in the old format. Even Congress confused the issue. It combined three bills into one act and because of an error in not replacing the word "act" with "section" also made it illegal for any alien to be naturalized who ever sold liquor in the U.S. Capitol building.[31] Due to these defective and variant procedures, Congress legalized all certificates issued under the 1903 law by an act of June 29, 1906.

Naturalization Laws 1906 - 1990

The Act of June 29, 1906, creating a Bureau of Immigration and Naturalization, had as its purpose "to provide for a uniform rule for the naturalization of aliens throughout the United States."[32] This resulting agency had authority for rule-making. With the Division of Naturalization's rule of August 25, 1906, a system to give "dignity, uniformity, and regularity" to the naturalization procedure began, effective September 27th. Its method was through the management, design, and control of forms. Rule Nine required "supplies of all blank forms and records . . . must be obtained exclusively from the Bureau of Immigration and Naturalization, Department of Commerce and Labor, those alone being official forms. No other forms shall be used."[33] By regulating the distribution of those forms and records, the agency could control the number of courts able to naturalize.

The bureaucracy created under the 1906 act continued to "purify" naturalization policy and process. The basic law was amended about twenty times from 1906 to 1940. This is approximately the same number of changes made in all naturalization laws, 1790-1906. Its rules went from four pages in 1906 to thirty-six pages in 1936. Federal courts clarified interpretation of the law. Significant amendments occurred in 1910, 1918, 1926, and 1929. Additional legislation affected the naturalization of women, veterans, and certain classes of aliens, such as Puerto Ricans and Filipinos. Other laws legalized past naturalization actions of courts.

The 1910 act permitted aliens who erroneously believed themselves citizens to be naturalized without a declaration of intention if they provided the court proof of U.S. residence for five years. The 1918 act addressed citizenship through military service and established procedures for naturalization of resident enemy aliens. An act of 1926 validated certificates of naturalization issued less than thirty days prior to an election.

The Act of March 2, 1929, was a major refinement of the 1906 law. It clarified the requirements for registry of aliens, including granting of certificates of arrival to aliens who had none if they arrived before June 3, 1921 (changed to July 1, 1924, by the Act of August 7, 1939), and could submit evidence. The law also made the certificate of arrival a part of the filing for a declaration of intention rather than the petition, as under the Act of 1906. Finally, it provided for certificates of derivative naturalization and required photographs to be affixed to both the declaration and the certificate of citizenship.

Starting in 1906, naturalization matters were handled by the Division of Naturalization under the Bureau of Immigration and Naturalization, Department of Commerce and Labor. In 1913, the division became the Bureau of Naturalization, Department of Labor, and continued until renamed in 1933 as the Immigration and Naturalization Service. This agency was transferred to the Department of Justice in 1940. Upon transfer and due to the Alien Registration Act of 1940, the volume of records grew exponentially. Each registry was given a number which became the basis for the "A" files. Beginning in 1944, the Immigration and Naturalization Service consolidated into one file the alien registration file, letters, the declaration of intention folder, and all other pertinent data. This process continued but was not retroactive. The service also had citizenship or "C" files based on certificates of citizenship filed since 1906. While the contents of the files themselves were centralized, beginning March 1, 1950, active records were decentralized to the various districts. By 1956, this procedure was complete. There is one centralized index to naturalization records, the "C" files, September 27, 1906 - April 1, 1956, in Washington, D.C. After that date, files, including naturalization records, have been incorporated in the decentralized "A" files located in the district office where the alien lived. Certificates of naturalization and related records have been microfilmed by the service.[34]

The Act of October 14, 1940, effective January 13, 1941, codified the amendments, additions, and supplemental laws of the Act of 1906. Basic procedures did not change significantly, although the forms, now issued by the Department of Justice, were numbered differently. This law, too, was amended. The naturalization code,[35] effective December 24, 1952, made the declaration of intention voluntary. It required the alien to file with the government an *Application to File Petition for Naturalization*, required a set of fingerprints, three photographs, and a *Biographic Information* form [see Illus. 13]. The Immigration and Naturalization Service investigated and, upon approval, authorized the alien to file his or her petition with the clerk of court. After a thirty day waiting period, a judicial hearing could be held, and the certificate of naturalization issued. Thus the court had the petition and the 3" by 5" certificate of naturalization stub index card as its record.

The Immigration and Naturalization Act of 1952, as amended, was replaced by the "Immigration Act of 1990."[36] This law, passed November 29, 1990, substantively amended the former one, including adding the provision of "administrative naturalization." It removed the courts from naturalizing aliens: Section 319(A) provided "the sole authority to naturalize persons as citizens of the United States is conferred upon the Attorney General." The law still provided for judicial review and permitted applicants to take their oaths of citizenship before "any District Court of the United States for any

State or by any court of record in any State having a seal, a clerk, and jurisdiction in actions in law or equity, or law and equity, in which the amount in controversy is unlimited. The jurisdiction of all courts in this subsection specified to administer the oath of allegiance shall extend only to persons resident with the respective jurisdiction of such courts." Section 408 made the 1990 Immigration Act effective upon passage but stated, " . . . no court shall have jurisdiction, under section 310(a) of the Immigration and Nationality Act, to naturalize a person unless a petition for naturalization with respect to that person has been filed with the court before October 1, 1991." Thus has ended a 201 year procedure for naturalization of aliens through the court system.

> Prior to the act of June 29,1906, the law placed no limitations on the vitality of a declaration, and the courts generally held that such paper filed prior to that date was not affected by the seven-year limitation placed by the act mentioned upon declarations filed under its provisions. A few of the courts, however, held that the seven-year limitation began to run against "old law" declarations from the date of operation of the new law, June 29, 1906, [sic] and then that all of such declarations became void seven years after that date, or on September 27, 1913. This view was sustained by the United States Supreme Court [in January 1918] . . . . As this decision invalidated many certificates already granted to worthy aliens, Congress in the Act of May 9, 1918, provided in section three thereof—that all certificates of naturalization granted by courts of competent jurisdiction prior to December 31,1918, upon petitions filed prior to January 31,1918, upon declarations of intention filed prior to September 27, 1906, are hereby declared to be valid . . . .[37]

Thus, the researcher can find petitions filed before January 31, 1918, supported by declarations of intention made prior to September 27, 1906. After January 31, 1918, however, all declarations had to be on Form 2202, under the Act of 1906.

The May 6, 1918, law also provided relief for those subjects of the Central Powers at war with the United States who were able to establish their American loyalty. Many aliens never completed their naturalization process but used the declaration of intention to vote, purchase real property, or file homestead entries.

> Cases have been reported of Unnaturalized foreign-born residents of the United States who have lived here over 70 years . . . . Instances were shown of those who had fought in the Civil War; where they had held offices of trust and responsibility, . . . such as members of State legislatures, mayors, judges, postmasters, and in other capacities. The registration required of persons born in the Central Powers who had not completed their American citizenship disclosed the most shocking state of affairs. Men and women who have their children and grandchildren in the military forces of the United States were disclosed as being not only aliens but enemy aliens.[38]

Under the Act of 1906, the petitioner for citizenship and his or her witnesses had to appear before the court to be examined under oath. This requirement was amended by an act of June 8, 1926, which permitted federal district court judges to "designate one or more examiners or officers of the

Immigration and Naturalization Service . . . to conduct preliminary hearings upon petitions for naturalization to such court."[39] This freed up the judge's time and made the operations of the Bureau more efficient. In addition, the March 4, 1929, amendment to the 1906 naturalization act required photographs be filed with the declaration. The changes were effective July 1, 1929. What did the bureaucrats do? They changed the forms.

These actions have caused much consternation among genealogists. First, naturalization literature has this event occurring from 1926 to 1932. Second, writers have implied that from this nebulously defined date onward, only federal courts continued to naturalize.[40] Neither observation is accurate. These amendments were used by many state and local trial courts as justification to discontinue naturalizing, especially if the volume of petitions was small.

The Bureau of Naturalization also was delayed in distributing new forms to the courts, so some took this opportunity to stop naturalizing. The government balanced, however, administrative convenience of reducing travel and time for their examiners with the feeling that closure of state courts exercising naturalization would be "a practical denial of the opportunity to become naturalized,"[41] due to cost of travel, loss of work, and witnesses' extra expense. Union County, Indiana, with a 1930 population of 6,017, continued to naturalize into the 1940's although located less than fifty miles from Cincinnati, Ohio. The Federal District Court at Terre Haute, Indiana, never naturalized, leaving that responsibility, to about 1958, with the local superior courts. Do not assume that no naturalization occurred in a county, large or small, after 1929. About a third to more than a half continued to do so for many years.[42] But by June 30, 1960, the number of courts was reduced to 684, many being federal courts.[43]

Except for the photograph, the substance of the new forms did not change significantly.[44] The format, however, did. Forms 2202 and 2204 became 2202 L-A and 2204 L-A and were issued in an 8" by 10-1/2" loose-leaf size. Post binders were used. Form 2207, the certificate of naturalization, continued in its single sheet format, in use since 1925. Preliminary worksheets for the declaration (2213) and petition (2214) were revised effective July 1, 1929, as A-2213 and A-2214. The affidavit of witness Form 2218 also changed.

Naturalizing courts continued to maintain the following records, each kept separately: the declaration of intention, Form 2202 L-A; the petition for naturalization, Form 2204 L-A, which also contained the oath of allegiance; and, if granted, the certificate of citizenship stub, which remained as a 3" by 5" index card. Also found are Form 2228, Order of the Court Granting Petitions and Form 2229, Order of the Court Denying Petitions. These records, along with any additional correspondence or information provided by the alien to the court and attached to his or her declaration and especially to his or her petition, constitute the naturalization records found in a typical courthouse after July 1, 1929.[45]

Naturalization Case Law

A little used "court of last resort" source for locating information on naturalization is case law, or the collective decisions of various appellate level courts. Many local trial court decisions have been appealed to a state or federal appellate level court, including legal issues regarding interpretation of the naturalization law generally, and specific issues involving an alien's right to own land, vote, or obtain benefits usually limited to citizens. These decisions collectively are reported separately for the federal government and for each state (but Delaware, Nevada, and Utah) in a series of publications, called Digests. A Digest takes appellate court decisions and arranges them according to over four hundred principles of law. Each set has a "Table of Cases" and a separate "Defendant-Plaintiff" table, where, by last name only, every case cited is indexed. Users should look under "aliens" and "citizens" and will have better luck if seeking an unusual surname. One can narrow the field, however, by noting only those cases under the surname that relate to the terms "aliens" or "citizens." The most comprehensive set of federal and state digests are published by West Publishing. The major series is called the "American Digest System" which traces case law from 1658 to the present. The "Century Digest" covers cases from 1658-1896 and the "First Decennial Digest" from 1897-1906. There is a collective "Table of Cases" and "Defendant-Plaintiff" table for this period. Thereafter, through 1976, there are "Decennial" editions. Since then, the series covers shorter periods of time. Federal court decisions are found in the *Federal Digest*, covering all federal courts, beginning in 1789.

A genealogist might approach West's *Indiana Digest, 2d*,[46] for Indiana appellate court cases from 1817 forward and consult the listing under "Naturalization." The cross reference will direct one to a series of decisions found under "Aliens." Here, under the subheading "Record, Certificate, and Evidence," is the reference: "**Ind. 1842**." One who has declared intention to become a citizen may take lands by purchase. Eldon v. Doe ex dem. Wynn, 6 Blackf. 341." This legal coding, explained in the front of each volume, refers to *Reports of Cases Argued and Determined in the Supreme Court of Judica-*

ture of the State of Indiana, by Isaac Blackford, volume VI, page 341. Each appellate opinion begins with a summary; for *Eldon v. Doe, on the Demise of Wynn and others,* one finds:

> "James Wynn, a native of England, emigrated to the United States in the year 1820, and on the 11th of October, 1820, in the Franklin Circuit Court in this State, declared his intention of becoming a citizen of the United States. In the report then made, he did not make registry of his wife and children. In the month of February, 1821, he purchased the premises named in the declaration, and died on the 23d of August, 1828, without taking the oath of allegiance. By his last will and testament, he devised to his daughter, Isabella, born in England, and then a member of his family, the land in controversy. After the death of her father, Isabella intermarried with Eldon, the appellant, by whom she had issue a son William Eldon. On the 26th of September, 1830, she died, and on the 20th of July, 1834, her son William also died. Eldon, the appellant, at the time of the death of his son William, was also an alien . . . ."[47]

While there are few such cases, knowing that various Digests exist, this is one class of records the genealogist cannot overlook. Many courthouse law libraries have the appropriate state digest and each state Supreme Court library contains federal and many state digests.

 # Unique 19th Century Procedures

REGISTRY

Genealogical literature suggests that early declarations of intention provide little useful data, a situation which supposedly did not change until printed forms and ledgers became popular in the 1850's or until after 1906. This is a misunderstanding of the naturalization process. Section 1 of the basic naturalization act of the nineteenth century provided not only "that he shall have declared . . . that it was, bona fide, his intention to become a citizen of the United States . . ." but section 2 repeated the registry requirement of the 1798 law and enlarged it to state:

> All free white persons, being aliens, who may arrive in the United States after the passage of this act [April 14, 1802], shall, in order to become citizens of the United States, make registry, and obtain certificates, in the following manner to wit: every person desirous of being naturalized shall, if of the age of twenty-one years, make report of himself; or if under the age of twenty-one years, or held in service, shall be reported by his parent, guardian, master or mistress, to the clerk of the district court of the district where such alien or aliens shall arrive, or to some other court of record of the United States, or of either of the territorial districts of the same, or of particular state; and such report shall ascertain the name, birthplace, age, nation and allegiance of each alien, together with the country whence he or she migrated, and the place of his or her intended settlement; and it shall be the duty of such clerk on receiving such report, to record the same in his office, and to grant to the person making such report . . . whenever he shall be required, a certificate . . . of such report and registry . . . .[48]

The Act of March 22, 1816, mandated:

> The certificate of report and registry, required as evidence of the time of arrival in the United States . . . and also a certificate . . . of the declaration of intention . . . shall be exhibited by every alien on his application to be admitted a citizen of the United States.[49]

For many Atlantic states' courts, the registry was *separate* from the declaration of intention. The National Archives (NARA) has three volumes of *Report and Registry of Aliens,* 1816-1828, for the Federal Circuit Court of Maryland, and NARA's Northeast Region, (Boston) has five volumes of similar registry order books for the Federal District Court at Boston, 1817-1845.[50] Even Edwards County, Illinois, created an *Alien Register,* 1817-1822.[51] Certificates of both the registry and declaration usually were issued when an alien moved [see Illus. 1]. The declaration of intention of Edward Reynolds, issued at Lancaster County, Pennsylvania, was filed in Indiana. If this declaration had been issued between 1798-1828, the genealogist would need to review Pennsylvania court records and seek the corresponding report and registry record [see Illus. 2 and 3].

The registry requirement of the 1802 law and its amendments were repealed by an act of May 24, 1828; but by the late 1820's, especially for non-coastal courts, the registry and declaration frequently were united as one document [see Illus. 4]. This combined report and declaration shows the richness of information such a record can have. If the declaration lacks the data elements required for registry and was issued between 1798 and 1828, one should research further to find the registry. Researchers should examine court records at port of entry or for different courts surrounding the one where the declaration was filed. The alien also may have filed his or her registry at about the same time he or she filed their declaration. Remember, the law required that both a registry and declaration had to be filed and recorded before granting a naturalization petition.

NATURALIZATION INVESTIGATIONS

You may have a declaration of intention or certificate of naturalization that exists nowhere else. It may be based upon fraud. In 1905, the Department of Justice reported on their investigation of naturalization activities and found fraud occurred for such reasons as employment, land ownership, or especially voting. Beginning in 1828 voting fraud involving naturalization was on the increase. The 1844 presidential election was so marked that a judge of the Lafayette, Louisiana, city court was impeached for illegally issuing naturalization papers.

> Colossal naturalization frauds [were] committed in New York, Pennsylvania, New Jersey, Ohio and other States in 1868 . . . . While the exact number of naturalization certificates issued out of the courts of New York for use at the election of 1868 can never be conclusively established, *owing to the fact that thousands were issued of which no record was made,* the aggregate has been fairly established as exceeding 58,000, of which fully 54,000 were issued by two judges in the supreme and superior courts in the month of October.[52]

New York did not have exclusive rights on fraud. Boston; Baltimore; St. Louis; Denver; Butte, Montana; Seattle; St. Paul, Minnesota; even Pella, Iowa; Barre, Vermont; and Biddleford, Maine had such scandals. An investigator in 1903 observed, "In one case I found that a judge had held an impromptu session of court late at night in a railroad station while waiting for a train for the purpose of conferring citizenship upon a number of aliens whose votes were needed at an election."[53] Congress

Commonwealth of Pennsylvania,

Lancaster County, ss.

I, ___Nathaniel W. Sample Jr.___ Prothonotary of the court of Common Pleas, in and for the county of Lancaster, in the second Judiciary district of Pennsylvania. DO CERTIFY, That at a Court of Common Pleas, holden at Lancaster for the county aforesaid, on the ___tenth___ day of ___October___ — one thousand eight hundred and twenty ___nine___

___Edward Reynolds___

a Native of ___Ireland___

declared, on oath, before said court, that it is BONA FIDE, his intention to become a *Citizen of the United States*, and to renounce, forever, all Allegiance and fidelity to any foreign Prince, Potentate, State or Sovereignty whatever, and particularly to ___George the Fourth King of the United Kingdom of Great Britain and Ireland his Heirs & successors forever___

In TESTIMONY whereof, I have hereunto set my hand and seal of the said court, the ___tenth___ day of ___October___ — in the year of our Lord, one thousand eight hundred and twenty ___nine___ —

___N. W. Sample Jr.___
___Pro'thy___

Illus. 1. OLD LAW DECLARATION OF INTENTION

This 1829 declaration of intention illustrates the form used from 1798 to 1828, when a separate registry form was required. Since it provides very little detail, one should also seek the registry record.

Illus. 2. REGISTRY AND DECLARATION

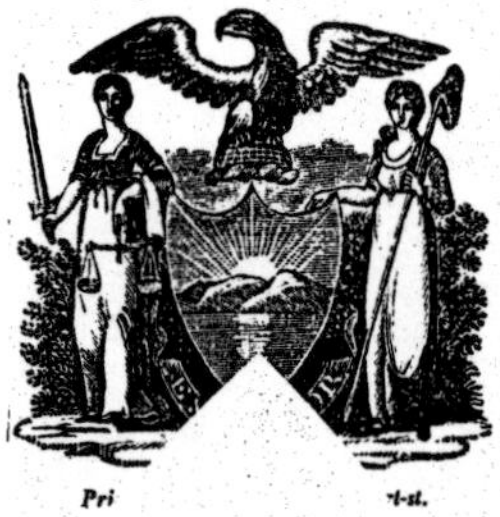

This 1824 Abstract of the Report and Registry of the alien, according to the 1798 and 1802 acts, combined registration with the declaration of intention. It also shows the wide variety of courts which naturalized in the nineteenth century. This abstract, made from the official record, was given to the alien when he moved.

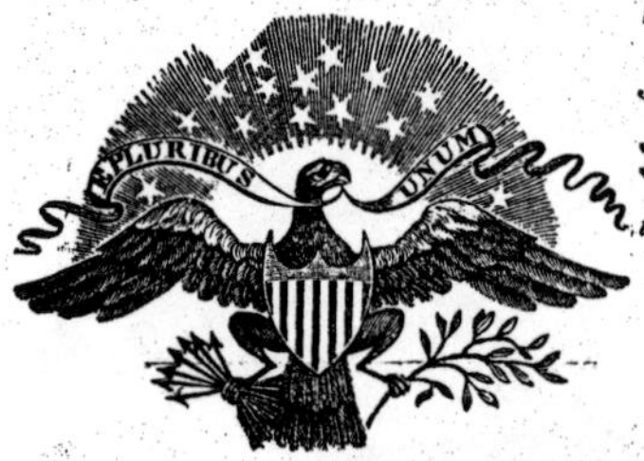

In pursuance of the Acts of Congress in such case made and provided *Nicholas Reichenbach* a free white person and an alien friend, desirous of being naturalized, makes report and registry of himself as follows:

Name.	Birthplace.	Age.	Nation.	Allegiance.	Whence he emigrated.	Time of arrival in the U. S.	Intended place of settlement.
Nicholas Reichenbach	*Maddadhäm*	28 July 1813	*Dukle Simburg Prussia*	*King of Prussia*	*Amsterdam*	*August 1837 in New York*	*Lehigh County Pa*

LEHIGH COUNTY, SS.

Nicholas Reichenbach being duly sworn, doth depose and say, that the above statement is correct, and that it is *bona fide* his intention to become a citizen of the United States, and to renounce forever all allegiance and fidelity to any prince, potentate, state or sovereignty whatever, and particularly to the *King of Prussia* of whom he is now a subject.

Nicholas Reichenbach

Sworn and subscribed before the prothonotary of the court of common pleas, at the borough of Allentown, in and for the county of Lehigh, the *first* day of *February* 1841

Attest} *John Farmela* Proth.

LEHIGH COUNTY, SS.

I *John Farmela* Prothonotary of the court of common pleas of Lehigh county, do certify the above to be a true copy of the report, registry, and declaration of intention, &c. of *Nicholas Reichenbach* as the same remains on file in my office. Witness my hand and seal of office this *first* day of *February* A.D. 1841

John Farmela Prothonotary.

Illus. 3. REGISTRY AND DECLARATION OF INTENTION

This 1841 registry and declaration of intention illustrates continued use of an obsolete form after the registry no longer was required.

State of Indiana
Franklin County } ss.

Be it Remembered that on the 22nd day of May A.D. 1834 Philip Hyde An alien, personally appeared before me Robert John Clerk of the Franklin Circuit Court for the County of Franklin aforesaid, and makes the following Report and declaration, to wit that he was born in the County of Lancaster in the Kingdom of Great Britain on the 8th day of April A.D. 1797, that he is upwards of thirty seven years of age; that he sailed from Liverpool a Sea port of said Kingdom on the 9th day of April 1830; that he arrived at New York in the State of New York in the United States of America on the 2nd day of June A.D. 1830 that he immediately left New York and arrived within about twelve miles of Dayton in the State of Ohio on the 29th day of June 1830. where he remained about eight or ten months, from whence he came and arrived in the County of Franklin and State of Indiana about the first of April 1831 and where he has since resided; and that he on oath declares, that it is bona fide his intention to become a citizen of the United States of America and to renounce forever all Allegiance & fidelity to every Foreign Prince, State, Potentate or sovereignty whatever & particularly to William the 4th King of the United Kingdom of Great Britain Ireland, Scotland & their dependencies —

Done before me at my office in
Brookville the 22d of May 1834 &
sworn to by the said Philip Hyde

Philip Hyde

Robert John Clk. F. C. C.

Illus. 4. DECLARATION OF INTENTION

This declaration combines questions asked under the old registry law with the declaration of intention. Listing of residences was required under the 1816 act. The official record of this declaration is found in the Franklin County, Indiana, Circuit Court Civil Order Book 5, page 237.

passed "An Act to Amend the Naturalization Laws and to Punish Crimes Against the Same," July 14, 1870. Although this increased the punishment for falsification of records in the naturalization process, it is quite possible to have evidence of an ancestor's naturalization not documented in the actual records of the supposed court which naturalized. The cause may be due to fraud. "Many of the holders of certificates issued in years gone by with a flagrant and obvious disregard of the requirements of the law were the victims rather than the perpetrators of the offenses which secured to them citizenship."[54]

The 1905 *Report to the President of the Commission on Naturalization* made observations significant to genealogists who require family data from naturalization records.

> The methods of making and keeping the naturalization records in both the Federal and State courts are as various as the procedure in such cases. Thus the declaration of intention in some courts consists merely of the bare statement of the intention and the name and allegiance of the alien, while in other courts it also includes a history of the alien . . . . In a majority of courts alien applicants are not required to make the declaration of intention required by law in the record of such declarations and in other courts he is. Previous to 1903 a majority of courts did not require petitions or affidavits; other courts did. Some courts keep a naturalization record separate from the other records; other courts include the naturalization record in the regular minutes of the court. Some records contain full histories of the aliens, but a majority of the records show only the name, nationality, oath of allegiance, and date of admission.[55]

An investigator of naturalization records for the Justice Department in 1903 observed:

> I find the naturalization records in many cases in a chaotic condition, many lost and destroyed, and some sold for old paper. Most of the records consist of merely the name and nativity of the alien with no means of identifying aliens of the same name . . . . In numerous cases I find aliens naturalized under initials instead of Christian names, surnames misspelled or changed entirely, and names of witnesses inserted in place of the alien naturalized [see Illus. 6] . . . . The examination of the records discloses the remarkable fact that never, since the first enactment of the naturalization laws, has any record been made in any court of the names of minor children who, under the operation of the statutes, were made citizens by the naturalization of their parents.[56]

One can see the need for uniformity and regularity in naturalization records to give the process dignity.

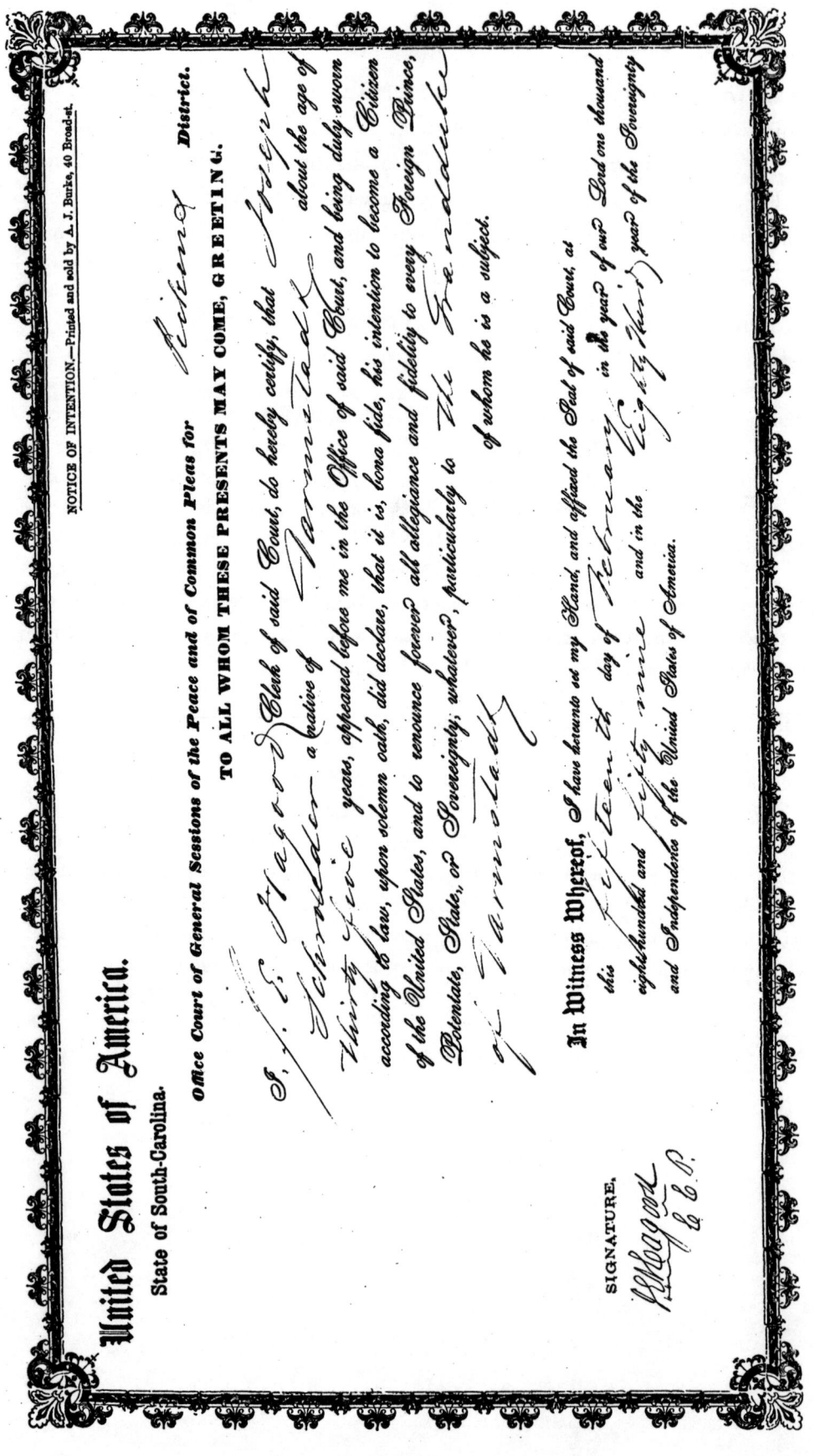

Illus. 5. NOTICE OF INTENTION

"Notice of Intention" for Joseph Schroeder, Pickens District, South Carolina, was filed in the Carroll County, Indiana Circuit Court when Schroeder petitioned for citizenship.

UNITED STATES OF AMERICA.

❧ DECLARATION OF INTENTION. ❧

STATE OF INDIANA, CLINTON COUNTY, SCT:

Martin Keefe states that he was born in *County of Kerry Ireland* ; that he is *Twenty four* years of age; that he is of the *Irish* nation; that he migrated from *Queenstown Ireland* on or about the *4ᵗʰ* day of *February* 1882, and arrived in the United States on the *17ᵗʰ* day of *February* 1882, that he intends settling in the United States, and owes allegiance to *Victoria Queen of Great Britain and Ireland and Empress of India*

and now declares upon oath, before the Clerk of the Clinton Circuit Court, that it is bona fide his intention to become a CITIZEN OF THE UNITED STATES, and to renounce forever, all allegiance and fidelity to any foreign Prince, Potentate, State or Sovereignty whatever, and particularly to *Victoria Queen of Great Britain and Ireland and Empress of India*

Signed: *Michael Keefe*

Subscribed and sworn to before me, the *19ᵗʰ* day of *September* 1887

Elwood Avery Clerk.
Clinton Circuit Court.

Filed and recorded *September 19ᵗʰ* 1887

Elwood Avery Clerk.

INDIANAPOLIS SENTINEL CO., Printers and Stationers.

Illus. 6. DECLARATION OF INTENTION SHOWING ERROR IN NAME
The clerk of court entered the declarant's name as "Martin," while Keefe signed his name "Michael." (Original court papers, Clerk of the Circuit Court, Clinton County, Indiana.)

Types of Records

The family historian seeks three citizenship records: the declaration of intention (first papers), the petition (second or final papers), and the certificate of citizenship. The quality and completeness of these records varied widely over time from court to court, especially in the nineteenth century.

"Prior to September 27, 1906, the effective date of the present basic naturalization statute, records of naturalization were kept only in the courts wherein the proceedings took place."[57] "The Government [after 1906] has complete records of all naturalization, and thus, in the case of destruction of the court records, is protected from illegal claims to citizenship, as the person naturalized is protected from the injuries in his personal and property rights."[58] Prior to 1906, the only duplicate record kept was a certified copy given to the alien. Thus, while major disasters, like the San Francisco earthquake and fire in 1906, resulted in a massive loss of naturalization records, citizenship records lost through courthouse fires often appear in another county since a copy of the declaration was required when the alien filed his or her petition. It became part of the files of the court hearing the petition [see Illus. 7].

With the exception of Mexico, the declaration was peculiar to the United States and was not required by state or federal law until 1795. It was a means of admitting an alien to citizenship on a step-by-step level, and to allow the granting of certain privileges, including the right to file a homestead claim for public lands, own real estate, and vote in certain states. During the Civil War and World War I, it gave the government the right to draft those aliens. Because of lack of uniformity of courts issuing declarations and of abuse in using them for fraudulent purposes, a 1905 study of then-existing naturalization procedures criticized requiring the filing of a declaration. It also served as a means to verify residence; but, as the report stated, this was not necessary because "since January 1, 1900, the Bureau of Immigration has had a record of every alien lawfully admitted to the United States."[59] Declarations were issued under a wide variety of forms and procedures, with content and validity varying greatly. The committee urged abandonment of the declaration of intention, a sugges-

State of Indiana

DeKalb County ss.   Comes now into the office of the Clerk of the DeKalb Circuit Court in said State, William Straus, and after being duly sworn, reports himself as follows to-wit:

I William Straus was born in Germany. I emigrated from Prussia sometime in April A.D. 1852 and arrived in New York in the United States on the tenth of June of the same year — I am aged twenty years past, and am by occupation a pedler. And while residing in Germany I owed allegiance to Frederick William King of Prussia

William Straus

Sworn to and subscribed before me this 18th day of June A.D. 1853.   John P. Widney Clk D.K. C.C.

Whereupon the said William Straus upon his solemn oath before said Clerk, declares his intention that it is his intention to become a citizen of the United States of America, and that he doth absolutely and entirely renounce and abjure all allegiance and fidelity to every foreign prince, potentate, state or sovereignty, and particularly to Frederick William King of Prussia, of whom he formerly was a subject.

Sworn and subscribed before me this 18th day of June A.D. 1853 —   William Straus

J.P. Widney Clk, DeKalb Circuit Court.

Illus. 7. CERTIFIED COPY OF DECLARATION OF INTENTION FILED BY ALIEN IN COUNTY WHOSE COURT RECORDS LATER WERE DESTROYED BY FIRE.
On June 18, 1854, William Straus filed his declaration in the DeKalb County, Indiana, courthouse. The court records were destroyed by fire in 1912. This certified copy was filed with his petition for citizenship in neighboring Noble County, and thus this information has been preserved.

tion only partially taken on December 24, 1952, when a new naturalization code went into effect, making the declaration voluntary since certain laws and regulations required aliens to have the declaration for employment in professional occupations.

> "Original declarations of intention become a part of the permanent records of the courts in which they are filed. The duplicates are filed in the Central Office and the triplicates are delivered to the aliens for retention until they petition for citizenship, at which time they are surrendered, attached to, and made a part of the naturalization petitions."[60]

The petition in the nineteenth century offers the least information and usually is the hardest to find. Most often it appears as an entry in the court's permanent official record. Relatively few courts used separate ledgers for petitions or "final papers." They rarely exist as originals or copies in the court's files of "loose papers." Only after 1906 do petitions become valuable for research.

> A Petition [for naturalization] is a large paper containing many dates, facts about the petitioner, and about his wife if married, and about his children if any; is verified by affidavit of two witnesses, . . . and is examined with his declaration of intention and must coincide with the latter paper and be sealed with the court seal.[61]

This is the nature of this record after 1906[62] and what the federal government hoped would have been the standard prior to the Act of 1906. Some courts in the nineteenth century met this standard; most did not.

The third major record found in both the nineteenth and twentieth centuries is the certificate of naturalization. "The title to citizenship is the recorded order of the court. The certificate is simply the conclusive evidence of such order."[63] "The certificate of naturalization is the written testimony by the court that these rights have been conferred. The court issues no other single document in attestation thereof."[64] What is the certificate's nature? As a court record, it was not kept as a separate or duplicate record until after September 27, 1906. Prior to that date the certificate was issued to the applicant. The court's record was the entry in its official proceedings. Even if a separate "Final Oath" or "Final Papers" ledger exists, there should be an entry in the court's minutes. Lack of uniformity in implementing naturalization by courts and clerks in the nineteenth century does not make this statement an absolute. If the court followed federal statute, the original "title to citizenship" should be enrolled in its official proceedings. If not recorded there, the applicant's certificate may have been issued fraudulently; or it could exist in separate records [see Illus. 8].

> Certificates of citizenship issued prior to the above-mentioned date [1906] were of various sizes and shapes, and were seemingly printed according to the fancy of the persons in each State charged with the preparation of the forms. The majority of the certificates contained no description of the naturalized person, lacked the signature of the person to whom it had been granted, and, in consequence, were easily transferable.[65]

THE STATE OF INDIANA, MARION COUNTY, SCT:

To all to whom these Presents shall come—Greeting:

KNOW YE, that at the *October* term, in the year eighteen hundred and forty *Six* of the *Circuit* Court of the County of Marion aforesaid, *Terence McManus* made the proof and took the oath to support the Constitution of the United States, and the oath of Allegiance required by law, before said Court, and was then, that is to say, on the *31st* day of *October* 184*6*, by said Court, duly admitted a Citizen of the United States.

In Witness of which, I, ROBERT B. DUNCAN, Clerk of said Court, hereunto affix the Seal thereof, and subscribe my name, at Indianapolis, this *26th* day of *December* 184*6*

R. B. Duncan

Illus. 8. "FINAL OATH"

This certificate of final oath is typical of many types given individuals upon naturalization in the nineteenth century.

The following steps became effective after September 26, 1906, as a result of the Act of June 29, 1906, as amended, or because of related legislation. These processes required a series of records to be created applicable to anyone who filed a declaration of intention or petition for citizenship, regardless of age or time of arrival in the United States, unless the individual met some exception. These record procedures applied to all courts in all states and were uniformly created:[66]

I. CERTIFICATE OF ARRIVAL, Forms # 526 & 526a and 160 [see Illus. 9].

The Certificate of Arrival "shows the date, place and manner of the alien's arrival into the United States." It was required of all aliens who arrived after June 29, 1906.[67] Until July 1, 1929, it became a part of the petition for naturalization; and the alien used a preliminary application form A-2214 for a certificate of arrival and a petition. After July 1, 1929, it was affixed to the declaration of intention; and the alien made application on Form A-2213, combined certificate of arrival and declaration of intention. If a certificate of arrival is in the possession of the family, it means that the alien did not file his or her petition before July 1, 1929, or did not file a declaration of intention after that date. Thus, citizenship was not complete.

II. CERTIFICATE OF REGISTRY, Form 658.

This was an alternative of the Certificate of Arrival and was permissible under the "Registry of Aliens Act," March 2, 1929, effective July 1. Designed to give permanent status to aliens residing in the United States who had no record of admission, it applied to those living in the United States prior to June 3, 1921 (later extended to those who arrived before July 1, 1924). The alien filed an application, which the Service investigated, and then issued a certificate to the alien (Form 658) who filed it with his or her declaration. Provisions of the 1906 Naturalization law requiring registry at all ports of

U. S. DEPARTMENT OF LABOR
BUREAU OF NATURALIZATION No. 11 33644

CERTIFICATE OF ARRIVAL

I HEREBY CERTIFY that the immigration records show that the alien named below arrived at the port, on the date, and in the manner shown, and was lawfully admitted to the United States of America for permanent residence.

Port of entry: New York, N.Y.
Name: Starros Stargin Bejas now Steve Starge Beja
Date: May 14, 1913.
Manner of arrival: SS. Athenia

I FURTHER CERTIFY that this certificate of arrival is issued under authority of, and in conformity with, the provisions of the Act of June 29, 1906, as amended, solely for the use of the alien herein named and only for naturalization purposes.

IN WITNESS WHEREOF, this Certificate of Arrival is issued

June 6, 1932.

BY DIRECTION OF THE SECRETARY OF LABOR.

Raymond F. Crist
Commissioner of Naturalization.

Form 160 C&W

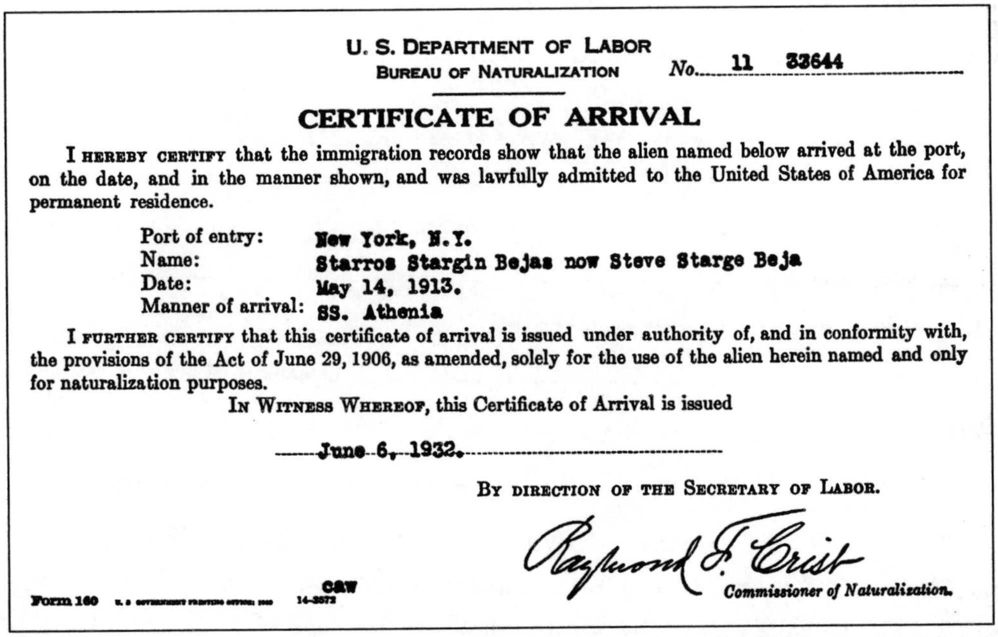

Illus. 9. SAMPLE OF A CERTIFICATE OF ARRIVAL

Form 2214
U. S. DEPARTMENT OF LABOR
NATURALIZATION SERVICE

☞ NOTE—FOR USE OF ALIENS WHO ARRIVED **BEFORE** JUNE 29, 1906

FACTS FOR PETITION FOR NATURALIZATION

Clerk of court and applicant should read these instructions carefully.

Clerks of courts should refuse to execute petitions for aliens who arrived in the United States after June 29, 1906, until certificate of arrival is furnished the clerk by the Bureau of Naturalization, after request of the alien on Form 2226. (See rule 5 of the Regulations.)

A copy of this form (2214) should be furnished by the clerk of court to each applicant for a petition for naturalization who arrived in this country **on or before June 29, 1906**, so that he can at his leisure fill in the answers to the questions.

The clerk of the court must collect the fee of $4 before he commences to fill out the petition.

No fee is chargeable for this blank or for the execution thereof by the clerk or deputy clerk.

After being filled out, this form is to be taken by the applicant to the clerk, to be used by him in properly filling out the petition.

Witnesses must be citizens of the United States. If any witness is a naturalized citizen, he must take his certificate of citizenship, or so-called second paper, to the court when the petition is filed, and also when it is heard by the court.

My name is _____
(Give true and original name in full.)

_____
(If any other name has been used in this country, it also should be given.)

1. I reside at _____
(Number and name of street.)

_____, _____, _____
(City or town.)   (County.)   (State.)

2. My occupation is _____

3. I was born on _____, _____, 1_____, at _____, _____
(Month.)   (Day.)   (Year.)   (City or town.)   (Country.)

4. I emigrated to the United States from _____ on
(State where you got on boat or train.)

or about _____, _____, 1_____, and arrived at _____ on
(Month.)   (Day.)   (Year.)   (Port of arrival in U. S.)

_____, _____, 1_____, on the vessel_____
(Month.)   (Day.)   (Year.)   (If arrival was otherwise than by vessel, the character of conveyance should be given.)

5. My declaration of intention was made on _____, _____, 1_____,
(Month.)   (Day.)   (Year.)

in the _____ Court, at _____, _____
(City or town.)   (State.)

(Hand your declaration of intention to the clerk of court with this form.)

6. I am _____ married. My {wife's / husband's} name is_____

She / He} was born on_____, _____, 1_____, at _____, _____
(Month.)   (Day.)   (Year.)   (City or town.)   (Country.)

and now resides at _____, _____, _____
(Number and street.)   (City or town.)   (State.)

If applicant is a married woman: Give date of marriage _____, _____, 1_____
(Month.)   (Day.)   (Year.)

Is husband a citizen?_____ If naturalized citizen, give date of his
(Yes or No.)

naturalization_____, _____, 1_____   14—1850   [OVER.]
(Month.)   (Day.)   (Year.)

Illus. 10. FACTS FOR PETITION FOR NATURALIZATION, Form 2214

Form 2214 was used by the Bureau of Naturalization to gather facts on aliens who arrived before June 29, 1906, the effective date of the law requiring Certificates of Arrival. This record was filed with the petitioner's folder in Washington, D. C. [See next page for reverse side.]

I have _____ children, as follows (give names in first spaces):

_____, born _____ day of _____, 1_____, at _____; resides at_____

_____, born _____ day of _____, 1_____, at _____; resides at _____

_____, born _____ day of _____, 1_____, at _____; resides at _____

_____, born _____ day of _____, 1_____, at _____; resides at _____

_____, born _____ day of _____, 1_____, at _____; resides at _____

_____, born _____ day of _____, 1_____, at _____; resides at _____

_____, born _____ day of _____, 1_____, at _____; resides at _____

7. I now owe allegiance to_____
   (Name of country of which you are now a subject.)

8. I am able to speak the English language.

9. I have resided continuously in the United States since_____ _____, 1_____, and
   (Month.) (Day.) (Year.)
   in the {Territory / State / District} of _____ since _____ _____, 1_____
   (Month.) (Day.) (Year.)

10. I have not heretofore made petition for naturalization; *or* I applied for naturalization to the_____

_____ Court at _____, _____, _____
                               (City or town.)   (State.)   (Month.)

_____, 1_____, which application was denied because_____
(Day.)   (Year.)

Give the names, occupations, and addresses of at least two citizens of the United States, each of whom has personal knowledge of so much of your residence during the past five years as you have spent in the State in which you now reside, and who will accompany you to the office of the clerk of court when you file your petition. If you have resided in any other State or States during the past five years, except the last year of that period, such residence may be proved at the hearing by depositions. Forms for depositions may be secured from the clerk when the petition is filed.

_____, _____, _____
   (Name.)   (Occupation.)   (Residence address.)

_____, _____, _____
   (Name.)   (Occupation.)   (Residence address.)

_____, _____, _____
   (Name.)   (Occupation.)   (Residence address.)

_____, _____, _____
   (Name.)   (Occupation.)   (Residence address.)

My witnesses have personal knowledge of my residence in the United States and the State since_____

_____ _____, 1_____   14—1850
   (Month.)   (Day.)   (Year.)

GOVERNMENT PRINTING OFFICE

Illus. 10A. Reverse side of Form 2214.

entry was not always met; for example, it was "overlooked by the administrators of the immigration law for a number of years at the ports of entry into the United States from Canada."[68]

III. DECLARATION OF INTENTION, Form 2202, 2202 L-A, Form N-315 [see Illus. 11, 12].

Under the 1906 act, the declaration was made before the clerk of court by an alien who had to be at least eighteen years old. There was no prescribed time period of residence in the United States before filing, and the alien filed a "Preliminary Form A-2213" with the Bureau. Three copies were made: (a) the original became part of the court's permanent record, (b) the duplicate was filed in the Bureau's central office in numerical and chronological order by court of issue,[69] and (c) the triplicate was given to the alien "for retention until they petition for citizenship at which time they are surrendered, attached to, and made a part of the Naturalization Petition." The Declaration (Form 2202, used between 1906-1929) was bound in ledgers of varying sizes and remained with the court. This is the official recording. Form 2203 was the perforated "duplicate" and "triplicate" of Form 2202, one being sent to the Bureau in Washington and the other given to the applicant. If a family has a declaration of intention issued after September 26, 1906, it may mean that the ancestor did not file a petition, or let it expire after seven years and had to file for a new declaration. One alien filed declarations in 1907, 1918, and 1940 before petitioning the court.

IV. PETITION FOR NATURALIZATION, Form 2204, 2204 L-A, N-405 [see Illus. 14, 15].

Before filing a petition for naturalization, the alien's declaration of intention must have been at least two years but not more than seven years old. He or she must have had five years of continuous residence in the United States and must have filed a preliminary petition on Form A-2214 with The Immigration and Naturalization Service (hereafter referred to as the Service), which performed a preliminary examination. Among information sought were: "It is necessary to ascertain the applicant's entire marital history, how many children he has, not only of his present marriage but of prior marriage if any, and where his wife and children reside."[70] Depositions also were taken, and these ultimately became part of the court's naturalization file on the individual. Upon completion of these steps, there was a final hearing in open court (for petitions filed prior to October 1, 1991) at least ninety days after filing the petition. As the last step, the petitioner took the oath of allegiance and renunciation of the former head of state.

Form 2204, 1906 - 1929, was the Petition for Naturalization, in ledgers of varying sizes. It is the official court and exclusive recording of the petition. (However, some trial courts still made an entry in its official ledger.) Beginning in 1920 it consisted of an original and duplicate, the latter being sent to Washington, replacing Form 2205, the latter being a duplicate, in single sheet form, containing the same data as Form 2204.

No. ....

ORIGINAL

UNITED STATES OF AMERICA

Department of Commerce and Labor
BUREAU OF IMMIGRATION AND NATURALIZATION
DIVISION OF NATURALIZATION

DECLARATION OF INTENTION

(Invalid for all purposes seven years after the date hereof)

.... } ss: In the .... Court

.... of ....

I, ..., aged .... years,

occupation ...., do declare on oath / affirm that my personal

description is: Color ...., complexion ...., height ____ feet ____ inches,

weight .... pounds, color of hair ...., color of eyes ....

other visible distinctive marks ....

....; I was born in ....

...., on the .... day of ...., anno

Domini 1............; I now reside at ....

I emigrated to the United States of America from ....

on the vessel* ....; my last

foreign residence was ....

It is my bona fide intention to renounce forever all allegiance and fidelity to any foreign

prince, potentate, state, or sovereignty, and particularly to ....

...., of which I am now a citizen / subject; I

arrived at the port of ...., in the

State / Territory / District of .... on or about the .... day

of ...., anno Domini 1............; I am not an anarchist; I am not a

polygamist nor a believer in the practice of polygamy; and it is my intention in good faith

to become a citizen of the United States of America and to permanently reside therein:

SO HELP ME GOD.

....
(Original signature of declarant.)

Subscribed and sworn to / affirmed before me this ....

[SEAL.] day of ...., anno Domini 19............

....,

Clerk of the .... *Court.*

By ...., ... *Clerk.*

*If the alien arrived otherwise than by vessel, the character of conveyance or name of transportation company should be given.

11—2526

Illus. 11. DECLARATION OF INTENTION, Form 2202
This form, issued by the Department of Commerce and Labor until 1913, and by its
successor, the Department of Labor, was in use from September 27, 1906, to July 1, 1929.

ORIGINAL

No. ....

UNITED STATES OF AMERICA

DECLARATION OF INTENTION
(Invalid for all purposes seven years after the date hereof)

.... } ss.: In the .... Court

.... of .... at ....

I, ...
(Full true name, without abbreviation, and any other name which has been used, must appear here)

now residing at ....
(Number and street) (City or town) (County) (State)

occupation ...., aged .... years, do declare on oath that my personal description is:

Sex ...., color ...., complexion ...., color of eyes ....

color of hair ...., height .... feet .... inches; weight .... pounds; visible distinctive marks

....

race ....; nationality ....

I was born in ...., on ....
(City or town) (Country) (Month) (Day) (Year)

I am .... married. The name of my wife or husband is ....

we were married on ...., at ....; she or he was
(Month) (Day) (Year) (City or town) (State or country)

born at ...., on .... entered the United States
(City or town) (State or country) (Month) (Day) (Year)

at ...., on .... for permanent residence therein, and now
(City or town) (State) (Month) (Day) (Year)

resides at .... I have .... children, and the name, date and place of birth,
(City or town) (State or country)

and place of residence of each of said children are as follows: ....

....

....

I have .... heretofore made a declaration of intention: Number ...., on ....
(Date)

at ....
(City or town) (State) (Name of court)

my last foreign residence was ....
(City or town) (Country)

I emigrated to the United States of America from ....
(City or town) (Country)

my lawful entry for permanent residence in the United States was at ....
(City or town) (State)

under the name of ...., on ....
(Month) (Day) (Year)

on the vessel ....
(If other than by vessel, state manner of arrival)

I will, before being admitted to citizenship, renounce forever all allegiance and fidelity to any foreign prince, potentate, state, or sovereignty, and particularly, by name, to the prince, potentate, state, or sovereignty of which I may be at the time of admission a citizen or subject; I am not an anarchist; I am not a polygamist nor a believer in the practice of polygamy; and it is my intention in good faith to become a citizen of the United States of America and to reside permanently therein; and I certify that the photograph affixed to the duplicate and triplicate hereof is a likeness of me: So HELP ME GOD.

[DO NOT ATTACH PHOTOGRAPH TO THIS COPY OF DECLARATION]

....
(Original signature of declarant without abbreviation, also alias, if used)

Subscribed and sworn to before me in the office of the Clerk of said Court,

at .... this .... day of ....

anno Domini 19........ Certification No. .... from the Commissioner of Naturalization showing the lawful entry of the declarant for permanent residence on the date stated above, has been received by me. The photograph affixed to the duplicate and triplicate hereof is a likeness of the declarant.

[SEAL]

....
Clerk of the .... Court.

By ...., Deputy Clerk.

Form 2202-L-A.
U. S. DEPARTMENT OF LABOR
NATURALIZATION SERVICE

14—2623   U. S. GOVERNMENT PRINTING OFFICE: 1932

Illus. 12. DECLARATION OF INTENTION, Form 2202 L-A
This form replaced the earlier Form 2202, effective July 1, 1929. It remained in use until January 13, 1941, when replaced by Form N-315.

INSTRUCTIONS: USE TYPEWRITER. BE SURE ALL COPIES ARE LEGIBLE. Failure to answer fully all questions delays action.
Do Not Remove Carbons. If typewriter is not available, print heavily in block letters with ball-point pen.
☆ U.S. GOVERNMENT PRINTING OFFICE: 1974-560-786

FORM G-325 (REV. 8-1-74) Y

BIOGRAPHIC
INFORMATION

UNITED STATES DEPARTMENT OF JUSTICE

Immigration and Naturalization Service

Form Approved
OMB No. 43-R436

(Family name)	(First name)	(Middle name)	☐ MALE ☐ FEMALE	BIRTHDATE (Mo.-Day-Yr.)	NATIONALITY	ALIEN REGISTRATION NO. (If any)
ALL OTHER NAMES USED (Including names by previous marriages)			CITY AND COUNTRY OF BIRTH			SOCIAL SECURITY NO. (If any)

	FAMILY NAME	FIRST NAME	DATE, CITY AND COUNTRY OF BIRTH (If known)	CITY AND COUNTRY OF RESIDENCE
FATHER				
MOTHER (Maiden name)				

HUSBAND (If none, so state) OR WIFE	FAMILY NAME (For wife, give maiden name)	FIRST NAME	BIRTHDATE	CITY & COUNTRY OF BIRTH	DATE OF MARRIAGE	PLACE OF MARRIAGE

FORMER HUSBANDS OR WIVES (If none, so state)

FAMILY NAME (For wife, give maiden name)	FIRST NAME	BIRTHDATE	DATE AND PLACE OF MARRIAGE	DATE AND PLACE OF TERMINATION OF MARRIAGE

APPLICANT'S RESIDENCE LAST FIVE YEARS. LIST PRESENT ADDRESS FIRST.

STREET AND NUMBER	CITY	PROVINCE OR STATE	COUNTRY	FROM MONTH	FROM YEAR	TO MONTH	TO YEAR
						PRESENT TIME	

APPLICANT'S LAST ADDRESS OUTSIDE THE UNITED STATES OF MORE THAN ONE YEAR.

STREET AND NUMBER	CITY	PROVINCE OR STATE	COUNTRY	FROM MONTH	FROM YEAR	TO MONTH	TO YEAR

APPLICANT'S EMPLOYMENT LAST FIVE YEARS. (IF NONE, SO STATE.) LIST PRESENT EMPLOYMENT FIRST.

FULL NAME AND ADDRESS OF EMPLOYER	OCCUPATION (Specify)	FROM MONTH	FROM YEAR	TO MONTH	TO YEAR
				PRESENT TIME	

Show below last occupation abroad if not shown above. (Include all information requested above.)

THIS FORM IS SUBMITTED IN CONNECTION WITH APPLICATION FOR:	SIGNATURE OF APPLICANT OR PETITIONER	DATE
☐ NATURALIZATION ☐ OTHER (SPECIFY) ☐ ADJUSTMENT OF STATUS		
Are all copies legible? ☐ Yes	IF YOUR NATIVE ALPHABET IS IN OTHER THAN ROMAN LETTERS, WRITE YOUR NAME IN YOUR NATIVE ALPHABET IN THIS SPACE:	

PENALTIES: SEVERE PENALTIES ARE PROVIDED BY LAW FOR KNOWINGLY AND WILLFULLY FALSIFYING OR CONCEALING A MATERIAL FACT.

APPLICANT:

BE SURE TO PUT YOUR NAME AND ALIEN REGISTRATION NUMBER IN
THE BOX OUTLINED BY HEAVY BORDER BELOW.

COMPLETE THIS BOX (Family name)	(Given name)	(Middle name)	(Alien registration number)

(OTHER AGENCY USE)	INS USE (Office of Origin)
	OFFICE CODE: TYPE OF CASE: DATE:

FORM G-325

(1) Ident.

Illus. 13. BIOGRAPHIC INFORMATION

This form replaced the declaration of intention and has been in use since December 24, 1952. The declaration of intention no longer was required, but permitted.

U. S. DEPARTMENT OF LABOR
NATURALIZATION SERVICE

ORIGINAL

No. ....

UNITED STATES OF AMERICA

PETITION FOR NATURALIZATION

To the Honorable the .... Court of .... at .... hereby filed, respectfully showeth:

The petition of ....

First. My place of residence is ....
(Give number, street, city or town, and State.)

Second. My occupation is ....

Third. I was born on the .... day of ...., anno Domini 1........ at ....

Fourth. I emigrated to the United States from .... on or about the .... day of .... anno Domini 1........, and arrived in the United States, at the port of .... on the .... day of .... anno Domini 1........ on the vessel ....
(If the alien arrived otherwise than by vessel, the character of conveyance or name of transportation company should be given.)

Fifth. I declared my intention to become a citizen of the United States on the .... day of ...., anno Domini 1........, in the .... Court of ....

Sixth. I am .... married. My wife's name is .... she was born on the .... day of ...., anno Domini 1........ at .... and now resides at ....
(Give number, street, city or town, and State.)
I have .... children, and the name, date and place of birth, and place of residence of each of said children is as follows: ....

Seventh. I am not a disbeliever in or opposed to organized government or a member of or affiliated with any organization or body of persons teaching disbelief in or opposed to organized government. I am not a polygamist nor a believer in the practice of polygamy. I am attached to the principles of the Constitution of the United States, and it is my intention to become a citizen of the United States and to renounce absolutely and forever all allegiance and fidelity to any foreign prince, potentate, state, or sovereignty, and particularly to .... of whom at this time I am a subject, and it is my intention to reside permanently in the United States.

Eighth. I am able to speak the English language.

Ninth. I have resided continuously in the United States of America for the term of five years at least immediately preceding the date of this petition, to wit, since the .... day of ...., anno Domini 1........, and in the State of .... continuously next preceding the date of this petition, since the .... day of ...., anno Domini 1........, being a residence within this State of at least one year next preceding the date of this petition.

Tenth. I have not heretofore made petition for citizenship to any court. (I made petition for citizenship to the .... Court of .... at .... on the .... day of .... anno Domini 1........, and the said petition was denied by the said Court for the following reasons and causes, to wit .... and the cause of such denial has since been cured or removed.)

Attached hereto and made a part of this petition are my declaration of intention to become a citizen of the United States and the certificate from the Department of Labor, together with my affidavit and the affidavits of the two verifying witnesses thereto, required by law. Wherefore your petitioner prays that he may be admitted a citizen of the United States of America.

....
(Complete and true signature of petitioner.)

Declaration of Intention No. .... and Certificate of Arrival No. .... from Department of Labor filed this .... day of ...., 191....

NOTE TO CLERK OF COURT.—If petitioner arrived in the United States on or before JUNE 29, 1906, strike out the words reading "and Certificate of Arrival No. .... from Department of Labor."

AFFIDAVITS OF PETITIONER AND WITNESSES

.... } ss:

The aforesaid petitioner being duly sworn, deposes and says that he is the petitioner in the above-entitled proceedings; that he has read the foregoing petition and knows the contents thereof; that the said petition is signed with his full, true name; that the same is true of his own knowledge, except as to matters therein stated to be alleged upon information and belief, and that as to those matters he believes it to be true.

....
(Complete and true signature of petitioner.)

.... occupation ...., residing at ....
and .... occupation ...., residing at ....
each being severally, duly, and respectively sworn, deposes and says that he is a citizen of the United States of America; that he has personally known ...., the petitioner above mentioned, to have resided in the United States continuously immediately preceding the date of filing his petition, since the .... day of ...., anno Domini 1........, and in the State in which the above-entitled petition is made continuously since the .... day of ...., anno Domini 1........, and that he has personal knowledge that the said petitioner is a person of good moral character, attached to the principles of the Constitution of the United States, and that the petitioner is in every way qualified, in his opinion, to be admitted a citizen of the United States.

....
(Signature of witness.)

....
(Signature of witness.)

Subscribed and sworn to before me by the above-named petitioner and witnesses in the office of the Clerk of said Court this .... day of ...., anno Domini 191.... [SEAL]

............, Clerk.
By ...., Deputy Clerk.

[OVER.]

Illus. 14. PETITION FOR NATURALIZATION, Form 2204
This form, in use from 1913 to June 30, 1929, replaced an earlier form distributed by the Department of Commerce and Labor, 1906-1913. The earlier form concluded with the information on "order of court admitting petitions" and information on petitioner's marriage and birth of children appeared on forms distributed after December, 1910. [See next page for reverse side of this form.]

IN THE MATTER OF THE PETITION OF

_____
TO BE ADMITTED A CITIZEN OF THE UNITED STATES OF AMERICA.

Filed _____, 19____

OATH OF ALLEGIANCE

I hereby declare, on oath, that I absolutely and entirely renounce and abjure all allegiance and fidelity to any foreign prince, potentate, state, or sovereignty, and particularly to _____ the _____ of _____ of whom I have heretofore been a subject; that I will support and defend the Constitution and laws of the United States of America against all enemies, foreign and domestic; and that I will bear true faith and allegiance to the same.

_____

Subscribed and sworn to before me, in open Court, this _____ day of _____, A. D. 19____

_____, Clerk.

NOTE.—In renunciation of title of nobility, add the following to the oath of allegiance before it is executed: "I further renounce the title of (give title), an order of nobility, which I have heretofore held."

ORDER OF COURT ADMITTING PETITIONER

Upon consideration of the petition of _____, and affidavits in support thereof, and further testimony taken in open Court, it is ordered that the said petitioner, who has taken the oath required by law, be, and hereby is, admitted to become a citizen of the United States of America, this _____ day of _____, A. D. 19____

(It is further ordered, upon consideration of the petition of the said _____, that his name be, and hereby is, changed to _____, under authority of the provisions of section 6 of the act approved June 29, 1906 (34 Stat. L., pt. 1, p. 596), as amended by the act approved March 4, 1913, entitled "An act to create a Department of Labor.")

By the Court:

_____, J

ORDER OF COURT DENYING PETITION

Upon consideration of the petition of _____ and the motion of _____ for the United States in open Court this _____ day of _____, 19____, it appearing that_____

THE SAID PETITION IS HEREBY DENIED.

_____, J

MEMORANDUM OF CONTINUANCES

REASONS FOR CONTINUANCE

Continued from _____, 19____

to _____, 19____

Continued from _____, 19____

to _____, 19____

NAMES OF SUBSTITUTED WITNESSES

_____, occupation _____, residing at _____

_____, occupation _____, residing at _____

Certificate of Naturalization, No. _____, issued on the _____ day of _____, A. D. 19____

14—916   [INSERT ON FOLLOWING LINES MARRIAGES AND BIRTHS OCCURRING AFTER PETITIONING AND BEFORE NATURALIZATION.]

Illus. 14A. Reverse side of Form 2204.

UNITED STATES OF AMERICA

No.

PETITION FOR NATURALIZATION

To the Honorable the _____ Court of _____ at _____

The petition of _____, hereby filed, respectfully shows:

(1) My place of residence is _____ (2) My occupation is _____

(3) I was born in _____ on _____ My race is _____

(4) I declared my intention to become a citizen of the United States on _____ in the _____

Court of _____, at _____

(5) I am _____ married. The name of my wife or husband is _____

we were married on _____ at _____; he was born at _____

on _____; entered the United States at _____ on _____ for permanent residence therein,

and now resides at _____; was _____ naturalized on _____

at _____ certificate No. _____ I have _____ children, and the name, date,

and place of birth, and place of residence of each of said children are as follows: _____

_____

_____

_____

(6) My last foreign residence was _____ I emigrated to the United States of

America from _____ My lawful entry for permanent residence in the United States

was at _____, under the name of _____

on _____, on the vessel _____
as shown by the certificate of my arrival attached hereto.

(7) I am not a disbeliever in or opposed to organized government or a member of or affiliated with any organization or body of persons teaching disbelief in or opposed to organized government. I am not a polygamist nor a believer in the practice of polygamy. I am attached to the principles of the Constitution of the United States and well disposed to the good order and happiness of the United States. It is my intention to become a citizen of the United States and to renounce absolutely and forever all allegiance and fidelity to any foreign prince, potentate, state, or sovereignty, of whom (which) at this time I am a subject (or citizen), and it is my intention to reside permanently in the United States. (8) I am able to speak the English language. (9) I have resided continuously in the United States of America for the term

of 5 years at least immediately preceding the date of this petition, to wit, since _____

and in the County of _____ this State, continuously next preceding the date of this petition, since

_____, being a residence within said county of at least 6 months next preceding the date of this petition.

(10) I have _____ heretofore made petition for naturalization: No. _____, on _____

at _____ and such petition was denied by that Court for the following reasons and causes, to wit:

_____
and the cause of such denial has since been cured or removed.

Attached hereto and made a part of this, my petition for naturalization, are my declaration of intention to become a citizen of the United States, certificate from the Department of Labor of my said arrival, and the affidavits of the two verifying witnesses required by law.

Wherefore, I, your petitioner, pray that I may be admitted a citizen of the United States of America, and that my name be changed to _____

_____

I, _____ do swear (affirm) that I know the contents of this petition for naturalization subscribed by me, that the same are true to the best of my own knowledge, except as to matters therein stated to be alleged upon information and belief, and that as to those matters I believe them to be true, and that this petition was signed by me with my full, true name: SO HELP ME GOD.

_____
(Complete and true signature of petitioner)

AFFIDAVITS OF WITNESSES

_____, occupation _____

residing at _____, and

_____, occupation _____

residing at _____
each being severally, duly, and respectively sworn, deposes and says: I am a citizen of the United States of America; I have personally known and have been acquainted

in the United States with _____, the petitioner above mentioned,

since _____ and that to my personal knowledge the petitioner has resided in the United States continuously preceding

the date of filing this petition, of which this affidavit is a part, to wit, since the date last mentioned and at _____

in the County of _____

this State, in which the above-entitled petition is made, continuously since _____, and that I have personal knowledge that the petitioner is and during all such periods has been a person of good moral character, attached to the principles of the Constitution of the United States, and well disposed to the good order and happiness of the United States, and in my opinion the petitioner is in every way qualified to be admitted a citizen of the United States.

I do swear (affirm) that the statements of fact I have made in this affidavit of this petition for naturalization subscribed by me are true to the best of my knowledge and belief.

_____   _____
(Signature of witness)   (Signature of witness)

Subscribed and sworn to before me by the above-named petitioner and witnesses in the respective forms of oath shown above in the office of Clerk of said Court at

_____ this _____ day of _____, Anno Domini 19 _____ I hereby certify that Certificate of Arrival No. _____

from the Department of Labor, showing the lawful entry for permanent residence of the petitioner above named, together with Declaration of Intention No. _____
of such petitioner, has been by me filed with, attached to, and made a part of this petition on this date.

_____
Clerk.   [SEAL]

By _____
Deputy

Illus. 15. PETITION FOR NATURALIZATION, Form 2204 L-A
This form replaced the earlier Form 2204, effective July 1, 1929. It remained in use
until January 13, 1941, when replaced by Form N-405.

V. CERTIFICATE OF CITIZENSHIP, Form 2207 [see Illus. 16, 17].

The certificate was issued in duplicate, with the original being given to the newly naturalized citizen and the copy filed in order under the serial number of the certificate from September 27, 1906 forward. "Certificates issued to evidence naturalization which occurred prior September 27, 1906, are consecutively numbered, the number being preceded by the letters, "OL," meaning "Old Law." After July 1, 1929, the certificate had the individual's picture affixed and showed change of name. Even after 1906 there continued to be unauthorized certificates of citizenship issued. "Such nondescript certifications are given out by clerks of many courts, notwithstanding the limitations of the law upon clerks of courts to issue only actual certificates of citizenship at naturalization. The issuance of such unstandardized fragmentary citizenship certificates is based upon the impression that the record of the court is public property and the clerk of the court is required to issue whatever excerpt, scrap, part, or paraphrase of record, however misleading, any individual may call for . . . . Such a paper has been judicially held to be a competent certificate of citizenship."[71]

Form 2207 was the Certificate of Naturalization, consisting of three parts: (1) the original, given to the naturalized citizen; (2) the duplicate, sent to Washington; and (3) a stub, retained by the court. Until October 25,1925 (and "until supplies were exhausted"), it consisted of books. After that date each certificate (original and duplicate) was loose, with the stub of the original serving as the court's index card. However, some clerks glued it into the Petition Record, rather than create a separate index.

VI. CERTIFICATE OF DERIVATIVE CITIZENSHIP

Since July 1, 1929, the Service could issue "Certificates of Derivative Citizenship," upon application Form 2400 or after 1940, N-600, to any individual who derived citizenship from spouse or parent, and who was twenty-one years of age. Statistics from the Service following 1929 reflect that relatively few received such certificates.

SUMMARY

Of these six major procedures, the declaration, petition, and certificate are those most sought, with records from the other steps becoming a part of one of these three records or else filed in Washington. With a bureaucratic procedure firmly entrenched, the genealogist benefits by finding the same format of record and ledgers from state to state and court to court. While these forms varied in number and content as the Bureau refined its operations, and while by 1913 the Bureau had 117 circular letters alone,[72] only a few additional forms require examination:

If an aliens's arrival in the United States was before June 29, 1906, the clerk of court prepared Form 2213 (Declaration of Intention) and Form 2214 (Petition). These duplicates of the court's copies of the declaration and petition were sent to Washington. The alien was required to prepare Form 2226, which was a worksheet for seeking a certificate of arrival and was in use from May, 1911

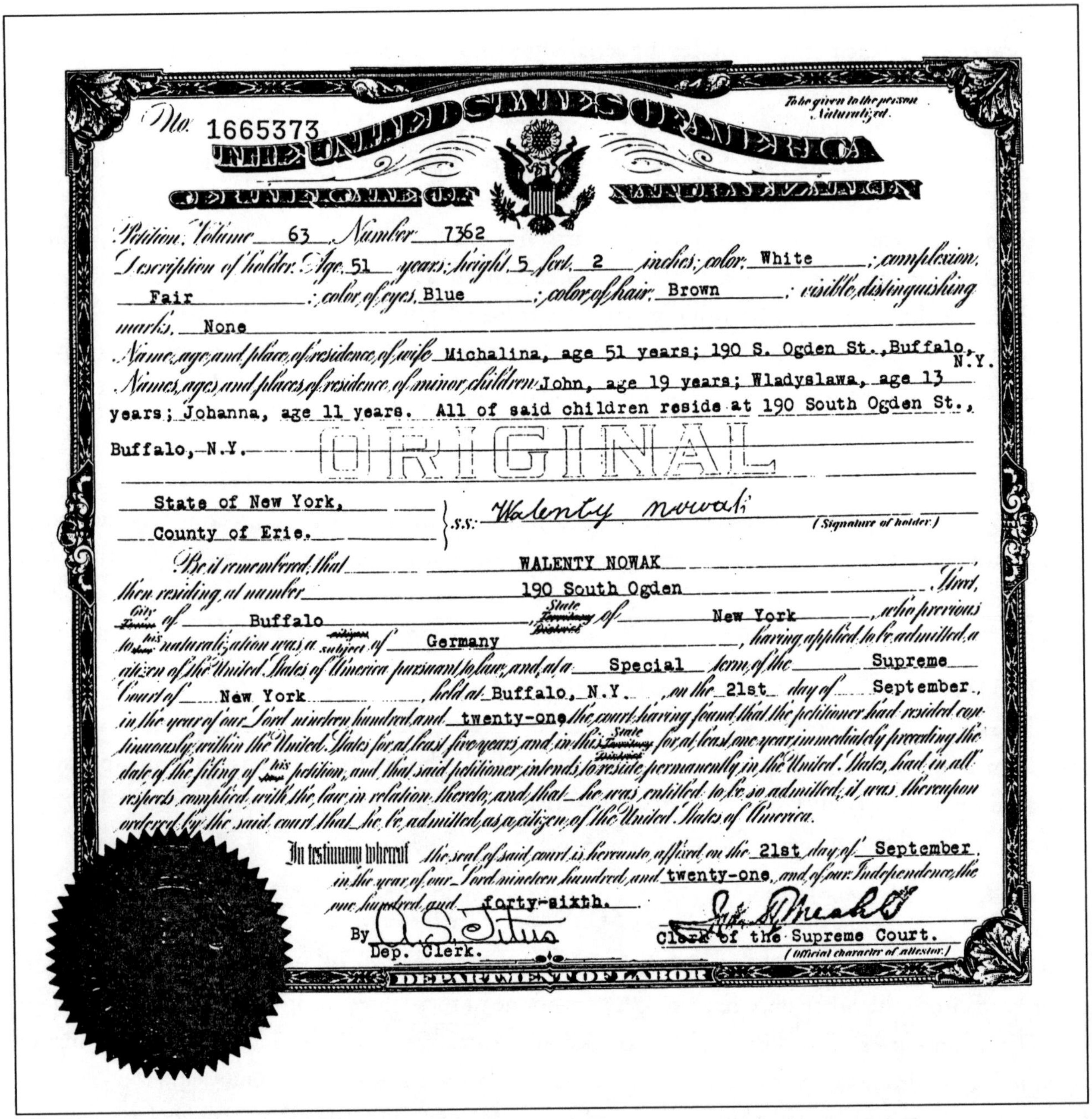

No. 1665373

To be given to the person Naturalized.

THE UNITED STATES OF AMERICA

CERTIFICATE OF NATURALIZATION

Petition, Volume 63 Number 7362

Description of holder: Age, 51 years; height, 5 feet, 2 inches; color, White; complexion, Fair; color of eyes, Blue; color of hair, Brown; visible distinguishing marks, None

Name, age and place of residence of wife Michalina, age 51 years; 190 S. Ogden St., Buffalo, N.Y.

Names, ages and places of residence of minor children John, age 19 years; Wladyslawa, age 13 years; Johanna, age 11 years. All of said children reside at 190 South Ogden St., Buffalo, N.Y.

ORIGINAL

State of New York,
County of Erie. } s.s: Walenty Nowak (Signature of holder.)

Be it remembered, that WALENTY NOWAK then residing at number 190 South Ogden Street, City of Buffalo State of New York, who previous to his naturalization was a subject of Germany, having applied to be admitted a citizen of the United States of America pursuant to law, and at a Special term of the Supreme Court of New York held at Buffalo, N.Y., on the 21st day of September, in the year of our Lord nineteen hundred and twenty-one the court having found that the petitioner had resided continuously within the United States for at least five years and in this State for at least one year immediately preceding the date of the filing of his petition, and that said petitioner intends to reside permanently in the United States, had in all respects complied with the law in relation thereto, and that he was entitled to be so admitted, it was thereupon ordered by the said court that he be admitted as a citizen of the United States of America.

In testimony whereof the seal of said court is hereunto affixed on the 21st day of September in the year of our Lord nineteen hundred and twenty-one, and of our Independence the one hundred and forty-sixth.

By A. S. Titus
Dep. Clerk.

Clerk of the Supreme Court.
(Official character of attestor.)

DEPARTMENT OF LABOR

Illus. 16. CERTIFICATE OF NATURALIZATION

This Certificate was issued to the naturalized citizen. A duplicate was sent to Washington, where it became part of the "C" file for all certificates of naturalization issued since September 27, 1906. (Original in the possession of private hands.)

DO NOT
WRITE BEYOND
BORDER LINE

Typewrite data on this certificate and stub. Type on stub surname first (ALL CAPITALS) followed by Christian and middle names in full without abbreviation (lower case).

No. 3147986

Name BEJA, STEVE STARGE

residing at 111 E. FRANKLIN ST., DELPHI, INDIANA

Age 39 years. Date of order of admission MAY 14, 1913

Date certificate issued JUNE 6, 1932. by the

CARROLL CIRCUIT Court at DELPHI, INDIANA

Petition N 209891

BEJA, STEVE STARGE
(Complete and true signature of holder)

DO NOT
WRITE BEYOND
BORDER LINE

ORIGINAL
STUB TO BE RETAINED AS
COURT RECORD

If clerk of court desires to file stub as a card index record, this stub may be trimmed so as to make a 3x5 card.

Illus. 17. STUB OF CERTIFICATE OF NATURALIZATION

The stub of the original certificate was first kept in the books of certificates until supplies were exhausted in 1925; then it served as the stub of individual sheets, trimmed to form an index card. The duplicate, sent to Washington, D. C. also was cut to be an index card to the government's "C" file of certificates.

to October, 1920. This form also was sent to Washington. These preliminary investigations were used to determine the facts stated by the alien [see Illus. 10 for sample Form 2214]. Forms 2215 and 2216 were certified copies of declarations and petitions used in support of homestead claims. Variations of these forms and others were used as conditions warranted. However, one should find the declaration books, petition ledgers, and certificate stubs each numbered consecutively for each court. For those with a large naturalization volume, petition ledgers have separate indices.

Not every one went through each of the major steps: filing a declaration, filing a petition, and receiving a certificate of naturalization based upon a judicial hearing and order. Some federal acts forgave the mandate of filing a declaration. Some alien residents felt that filing the declaration was all that was required. Until September 27, 1906, there was no statute of limitations on its validity. Others obtained that "first paper" with the plan of returning to their homeland with a most favored citizen classification. Some participated in naturalization fraud for political or employment reasons. While the number of states which granted aliens the franchise varied in the nineteenth century, in 1905 nine states permitted aliens to vote in general elections upon proof of filing a declaration of intention.[73] These were Arkansas, Indiana, Kansas, Michigan, Missouri, Nebraska, Oregon, Texas, and Wisconsin. For the general election year of 1912, in Indiana courts 4,351 aliens filed declarations of intention; 809 filed petitions for naturalization; and 715 received certificates. In Kansas, the figures were 1,559 declarations, 660 petitions, and 282 certificates. In North Dakota, on the other hand, where alien voting was not permitted, 1,762 declarations and 2,135 petitions were filed; and 2,151 certificates of citizenship were granted.[74] The Division of Naturalization estimated that from two to two-and-a-half times more declarations were filed than certificates were issued for citizenship.[75]

A David Duell was born in England March 17, 1828, and arrived at the port of New York in March, 1829. He filed his declaration[76] October 17, 1912, at the age of 84 [see Illus. 18]. Why? What motivated him to do so? No evidence survives as to his reason, but the answer may lie in understanding laws in place in Indiana in 1912.[77] Although there is no evidence, he probably came with his parents. If so, his father may never have been naturalized or at least while Duell was under twenty-one, since he would have acquired derivative citizenship. Indiana, in 1912, required documentation of one's declaration of intention, through a newly passed voter registration system. While one will never know why, there may be a link between Indiana's voter registration law and Duell's filing a declaration. Knowledge of land ownership laws, voting rights, occupational licensing, and other requirements that affected one's status as a citizen can lead to locating a naturalization, even for a person who had been a resident for 83 years [see Illus. 19].

No. 27

ORIGINAL

UNITED STATES OF AMERICA

Department of Commerce and Labor
BUREAU OF IMMIGRATION AND NATURALIZATION
DIVISION OF NATURALIZATION

DECLARATION OF INTENTION

(Invalid for all purposes seven years after the date hereof)

State of Indiana } ss: In the _Circuit_ Court
Putnam Co   of _Putnam County_

I, _David Duell_ , aged _84_ years,
occupation _Farmer_ do declare on oath affirm that my personal
description is: Color _white_ , complexion _fair_ , height _5_ feet _9_ inches,
weight _150_ pounds, color of hair _Gray_ , color of eyes _Brown_
other visible distinctive marks _____
_____ ; I was born in _England_
_____ , on the _17_ day of _March_ , anno
Domini 1_828_ ; I now reside at _Reelsville Indiana_
I emigrated to the United States of America from _England_
on the vessel* _____ ; my last
foreign residence was _England_
It is my bona fide intention to renounce forever all allegiance and fidelity to any foreign
prince, potentate, state, or sovereignty, and particularly to _George V_
_____ , of which I am now a citizen subject ; I
arrived at the port of _New York_ , in the
State Territory of _New York_ on or about the _____ day
District of _March_ , anno Domini 1_829_ ; I am not an anarchist; I am not a
polygamist nor a believer in the practice of polygamy ; and it is my intention in good faith
to become a citizen of the United States of America and to permanently reside therein:
SO HELP ME GOD.

David Duell
(Original signature of declarant.)

Subscribed and sworn to affirmed before me this _17th_

[SEAL.]

day of _October_ , anno Domini 19_12_

Arthur J Hamrick ,
Clerk of the _Putnam_ Court.
By _Arthur J Hamrick_ Clerk.

*If the alien arrived otherwise than by vessel, the character of conveyance or name of transportation company should be given.

11—2526

Illus. 18. DECLARATION OF INTENTION OF DAVID DUELL
Declaration of an 84 year old probably filed to permit him to vote under Indiana's Voter Registration Statute.

IMPORTANT NOTE.—The voter should fill out this blank, all but the number, sign in English if he be able to write his name in English, if not, then in any language that he may be able to write, take with him on the day of Registration to the place thereof in his Precinct and deliver in person to the Board of Registration. If the voter is not able to write he may procure some resident of the Township to write his name for him and he shall then make his mark. The person so writing his name shall also write his own name on this application as attesting witness.

The first session of the Board of Registration will be held on THURSDAY, THE 180th DAY preceding the election, BEING THE SECOND THURSDAY, THE 9th DAY OF MAY, 1912. WRITE WITH PEN AND INK. THIS BLANK IS GOOD FOR MAY REGISTRATION ONLY.

Application for Registration of FOREIGN BORN Naturalized Voter.

No. *37*

MAY SESSION.

Date *May 9* 1912.

My name is *Wm Knapp*, I reside in *Second* Precinct,

_____ Ward,* _____, in *Highland* Township,

Franklin County, Indiana, at No.* _____, _____ Street,*

On my own Farm

I was *62* years of age on the *First* day of *July* 1917

I was born in *Wirtemberg Germany* arrived in *U.S. Oct 2 1856*

I was naturalized under the laws of the United States at *Cincinnati*

Hamilton Co. Ohio on the *27* day of *September 1892*

Signature *Wm Knapp*

* If the residence is situate outside of a town or city, give the name of the owner, or reputed owner, of the real estate on which the applicant resides; if inside of a town or city that has street numbers give the street number and name of the street, also the name of the town or city: if inside of a town or city that has no street numbers give the character of the house, whether frame, brick or other material, one or more stories, on what street or alley, and on which side thereof, and the nearest cross streets between which it is situate and the name of the town or city.

Illus. 19. VOTER REGISTRATION

Example of form used for voter registration at the turn of the century. Voter registration records are a good source of citizenship information.

# Derivative Citizenship

Development and changes in law, policy, and uniformity of procedure concerning derivative citizenship are of equal interest.[78] Derivative citizenship is that based upon citizenship of another or upon some service the applicant performed, causing the naturalization process not to follow every step generally required of aliens. Naturalization proceedings, as discussed here, are those dependent upon another individual, and not group naturalization, as granted to residents of a territory and to classes of people, such as American Indians or the Chinese. Derivative citizenship of children and wives serve as examples.

Minors have become citizens automatically by naturalization of the parent since the Act of March 26, 1790: "The children of such persons so naturalized, dwelling within the United States, being under the age of twenty-one years at the time of such naturalization, shall also be considered as citizens of the United States." This language reappeared in the naturalization statutes of 1795 and 1802, the latter not being repealed until 1940.[79] The Act of March 26, 1804, permitted widows and minor children of a deceased applicant, who had filed his declaration of intention but who died before the naturalization proceeding, to be declared citizens upon taking the oath prescribed by law. This language also appeared in the 1906 law. An act of May 26, 1824, provided that minor aliens, who had lived in the United States three years before age 21 and for two years thereafter, could make application for naturalization without a previous declaration of intention but were required to file a declaration at the time of their admission [see Illus. 20]. They also had to conform with other aspects of the law. This act, subject to much abuse in the nineteenth century, was repealed by the law of 1906. An act of February 24, 1911, required no declaration of intention by the wife and minor children of an alien who filed his declaration, if after that time he became insane and she filed a homestead entry. Other requirements were to be followed. These and later laws permitted citizenship automatically or excused the requirement for a minor filing a declaration of intention on his or her behalf.

The Bureau of Naturalization continually complained about lack of documentation for those whose citizenship derived from another. While there are no definitive sources the genealogist can consult, the following may assist in documenting male minor children's citizenship due to a parent:

- Under the 1824 law, the child had to file his declaration of intention with his petition.

- After 1906, the name and age appeared on the petition for naturalization and certificate of citizenship upon which derivative citizenship could be based. (Most likely the certificate was issued after July 1929.)

- Selective Service World War I Draft Registration Cards. All three registrations asked if naturalized, had filed his declaration, or was an alien. The third asked if registrant was a citizen by father's naturalization before he reached his majority.

- Voter registration records found in local courthouses, especially for the early twentieth century when there was an effort to require better documentation of citizenship status for voters.

A similar structure existed for spouses of naturalized men. From 1790 to 1922 the wife became naturalized upon citizenship conferred to her husband; no separate filings were required. An act of February 10, 1855, stated "any woman who might lawfully be naturalized under the existing laws, married, or who shall be married to a citizen of the United States, shall be deemed and taken to be a

Illus. 20. MINOR'S PETITION

Example of a minor's petition for citizenship, including the declaration, as a result of the 1824 statute.
Original found in Clinton County, Indiana, Circuit Court Civil Order Book 3, page 45.

citizen."[80] This law was repealed by an act of September 22, 1922, which removed such marriage as the means for citizenship. A married woman now had to be naturalized on her own.

Biographical data, prior to 1906, except for the Registry period, 1798-1828, rarely existed for children and spouses in declarations and petitions. It became mandatory after September 27, 1906. The name, age, birth date and place, marriage date and place, and the names of minor children, their birth dates and places and residences were required. The 1915 *Annual Report* of the Bureau of Naturalization estimated that there were five to a typical family, so that while only 100,000 received certificates of naturalization yearly, 400,000 more became citizens.[81]

An amendment to the 1906 law by the Act of March 2, 1929, concerning issuance of certificates of naturalization brought this comment in the Bureau's 1929 *Annual Report:*

> A departure was incorporated in the legislation from the historical course pursued since the passage of the naturalization act of 1790. At no time heretofore has a certificate of citizenship been authorized to be issued to any naturalized citizen other than the one who petitioned to the court for admission to citizenship. In the past the wife of the naturalized citizen became a citizen upon his naturalization. No certificate of citizenship was authorized to be given to her. At all times minor children of the parent naturalized have likewise obtained citizenship, but no certificate of citizenship was ever authorized to be issued to any of them . . . .Thus, for the first time in the history of the country, those who derive or have heretofore derived citizenship through the naturalization of the petitioner for citizenship may themselves receive certificates of citizenship.[82]

The 1929 amendment was discretionary and required that for these citizens an oath of allegiance be made for the first time. The Bureau of Naturalization received 1,640 applications for certificates of derivative citizenship during the first year under the new law. Two years later the number was 788. Thus, while this modern law was not used by a large number deriving citizenship from others, its existence is worth noting, as an additional source for that elusive ancestor.[83]

The Commissioner of Naturalization commented on this problem of citizens of foreign birth who had not secured citizenship through the naturalization process:

> "They derived their citizenship through the naturalization of their parents or through the naturalization of their husbands prior to the Act of September 22, 1922. Prior to July 1,1927, there had been 2,385,906 persons naturalized upon petitions under the operation of the Act of June 29, 1906. Just how many citizens of the United States are now living who derived their citizenship through the naturalization of the father or husband it is not possible to say."[84]

 # Citizenship Based on Military Service

VETERANS' NATURALIZATION PROCEDURES

Special considerations regarding the naturalization process were given veterans. An act of July 17, 1862, permitted

> any alien, of the age of twenty-one years and upwards, who has enlisted, or may enlist in the armies of the United States, either the regular or the volunteer forces, and has been, or may be hereafter, honorably discharged, shall be admitted to become a citizen of the United States, upon his petition, without any previous declaration of intention to become such; and he shall not be required to prove more than one year's residence.[85]

While this legislation was used to induce aliens to enlist for the Civil War, it applied to any conflict, including Indian and the Spanish-American wars. One would not find any declaration made but would find proof of residence, good moral character, and of his honorable discharge. After 1906, in addition to the petition, the stub of the certificate of naturalization also was to note such discharge. The special 1890 U.S. Census showed that there were surviving 172,573 foreign-born white veterans.[86] Thus, the law applied to a large number of aliens.

The Act of July 26, 1894, extended the same privilege of citizenship without filing a declaration of intention to those who had "served five consecutive years in the United States Navy or one enlistment in the United States Marine Corps" and who also had been honorably discharged.[87]

Congress permitted naturalization of a seaman who served three years on a merchant vessel of the United States after filing his declaration of intention due to his lack of residence in a single place. This act of June 7, 1872, required proof of his certificate of discharge as well as his declaration of intention before granting citizenship. Other classes of service were not covered, such as government employees who served on vessels of the War Department, Coast and Geodetic Survey, and the lighthouse establishment, though their duties also prevented them from complying with the residency provision of the naturalization law.[88]

In contrast to this benefit, the Act of August 1, 1894, required among other criteria, that "no person (except an Indian) who is not a citizen of the United States, or who has not made legal declaration of his intention to become a citizen . . . shall be enlisted" in the Army of the United States during time of peace.[89]

During World War I codification of the various laws regarding naturalization of soldiers, sailors, and veterans was required. The Act of May 9, 1918, consolidated the many laws relating to naturalization of aliens who had served in the military or related services. It also significantly affected aliens fighting in that war. "Any alien serving in the military or naval service of the United States during the time this country is engaged in the present war may file his petition for naturalization without making the preliminary declaration of intention and without proof of the required five years residence within the United States."[90] "The Provost Marshal General, in his report of December 20, 1917, showed 123,277 foreigners in the National Army" and gave "a possibility of 487,713 aliens" under the age of 21 as additional soldiers.[91] Between May 9, 1918, and June 30, 1919, 192,328 aliens were so naturalized. "The Act of May 9, 1918, provided for the immediate naturalization of alien soldiers, eliminating the required declaration of intention, the certificate of arrival, and proof of residence."[92] These soldiers were naturalized at military camps and nearby courts[93] and not at their or their families' legal residences. Acts of July 19, 1919 and May 26, 1926 extended the provisions of the 1918 law. The 1940 Nationality Act continued such arrangements regarding veterans to those serving in World War II as did later laws to veterans of more recent conflicts. Thus, special naturalization features have existed for applicants who had served honorably during World War I (April 16, 1917 - November 11, 1918), World War II (September 1, 1939 - December 31, 1946), the Korean Conflict (June 25, 1950 - July 1, 1955), the Vietnam Conflict (February 28, 1961 - October 15, 1978), and Operation Desert Shield/Desert Storm (August 28, 1990 - April 11, 1991).[94]

FOREIGN-BORN WORLD WAR I DRAFT REGISTRATION

More than one in five who registered for the draft were foreign-born, representing over 3.8 million aliens and 1.3 million naturalized citizens. These men were born between 1873 and 1900. There were three registrations, each using a distinct registration card. The originals are maintained by the NARA's Southeast Region (Atlanta) and have been microfilmed by the Genealogical Society of Utah, consisting of 4, 382 rolls of 16mm microfilm. Local draft boards represented a county; or, if more than 30,000 population, additional boards were created. For large cities, there could be two to over one hundred local registration boards. To locate an individual requires diligence since there are no indexes. The last roll of film for each state is entitled "Indians, Prisoners, Insane, in Hospital, and *Late Registrants*." If a relative is not found in the registration district that incorporates his legal residence, consult this roll of microfilm also.

There were three primary registration dates: June 5, 1917, June 5, 1918, and September 12, 1918. Different registration cards, requiring distinctive information, were used for each registration cycle. Information required by each included name in full, date of birth, if the registrant was native-born, naturalized, an alien, who made his declaration of intention, and if not a citizen, of what nation he was a citizen or subject [see Illus. 21]. The second registration asked for exact birthplace of father [see Illus. 22]. The third registration asked if the registrant was a non-declarant and if he became a citizen by his father's naturalization [see Illus. 23]. Thus for those who registered September 12, 1918, and whose father had become a citizen before that date, this question would give the family historian information that naturalization occurred and could lead to other records.

To better understand their value, knowledge of this registration process and who it affected is helpful. Under provision of international law then in effect, an "alien friend" who was domiciled in, or deemed a permanent resident of, a country could be compelled to serve in its military. Filing a declaration of intention, thus becoming a "declarant," was conclusive evidence that an alien was a permanent resident and subject to the draft. Congress, in the Selection Service Act, based the draft "upon liability to military service of all male citizens, or male persons not enemy aliens who have declared their intention to become citizens."[95] The means to determine this liability was through registration. While enemy aliens could not be compelled to serve, they still were bound to register. By understanding this distinction, the genealogist can assume that virtually all foreign-born males, from September 1873 through September 1900, were registered.

The following statistical breakdown[96] provides information on the number of aliens, those who had filed a declaration of intention, and those who were naturalized on each registration date.

FIRST REGISTRATION, June 5, 1917, for males born June 6, 1887 - June 5, 1896:

Aliens registered	1,616,812
Aliens who had declared	518,216
Naturalized citizens	259,470

SECOND REGISTRATION, June 5, 1918, for males born June 6, 1896 - June 5, 1897 & supplemental Registration August 24, 1918 for males born June 6, 1897 - August 24, 1897:

Aliens registered	86,194
Aliens who had declared	20,147
Naturalized citizens	11,215

THIRD REGISTRATION, September 12, 1918, for males born September 13, 1872 - June 5, 1887 & August 25, 1897 - September 12,1900:

Aliens registered	2,174,077
Aliens who had declared	731,819
Naturalized citizens	1,065,982

The total represents 3,877,083 aliens and 1,336,987 naturalized citizens, or 5,214,050 foreign-born out of a total of 23,908,576 who registered in the 48 states and the District of Columbia. This is 21.8% of these World War I registrants.

These aliens fall into three categories:

(1) allied (cobelligerents)	2,228,980
(2) neutrals	636,601
(3) enemy aliens[97]	1,011,502

Because a large number of enemy aliens represent nationalities having great genealogical interest, further commentary is necessary. An enemy alien was one whose birth occurred in a country at war with the United States. These included both "declarant" and "non-declarant" of their intention to become citizens but excluded those already naturalized. During World War I, there were four groups of enemy aliens:

(a)	Germany, at war April 7, 1917	158,809
(b)	Austria-Hungary, at war November 11, 1917	751,212
(c)	Turkey and	81,608
	Bulgaria	19,873
	[No formal declaration of war but considered as enemy aliens.]	

(d) Countries controlled by those at war with the United States (Yugoslavia, Czechoslovakia, Rumania). Aliens from these counties were considered enemy aliens until Congress created the Slavic Legion July 10, 1918.

Form 1	553	REGISTRATION CARD	No. 96	

1245

1 Name in full ...... *Fritz Oscar Olson* 25
(Given name) (Family name)

2 Home address *601 E 12th St. Portland Ore.*
(No.) (Street) (City) (State)

3 Date of birth ...... *February 28 1892*
(Month) (Day) (Year)

4 Are you (1) a natural-born citizen, (2) a naturalized citizen, (3) an alien, (4) or have you declared your intention (specify which)? *Declarant.*

5 Where were you born? *Nygaby* *Sweden*
(Town) (State) (Nation)

6 If not a citizen, of what country are you a citizen or subject? *Sweden*

7 What is your present trade, occupation, or office? *Carpenter*

8 By whom employed? *Grant Smith Co.*
Where employed? *Bowdoin Mont*

9 Have you a father, mother, wife, child under 12, or a sister or brother under 12, solely dependent on you for support (specify which)? *No*

10 Married or single (which)? *Single* Race (specify which): *Cau*

11 What military service have you had? Rank *None*; branch ......
years ......; Nation or State ......

12 Do you claim exemption from draft (specify grounds)? *None*

I affirm that I have verified above answers and that they are true.

......
(Signature or mark)

Illus. 21. SELECTIVE SERVICE REGISTRATION CARD, FIRST CALL, JUNE 5, 1917

Serial No. 150   67a   Registration No. 150

1	Name in full Andrew (Citizen name) Rosi (Family name)	21

2 Home address 329 E. 8th St., Portland, Ore.
    (No.)   (Street)   (City or town)   (State)

3 Date of birth July (Month) 6th (Day) 1897 (Year)

4 Where were you born? Genoa (City or town) Italy (Nation)

5 I am { 1. ~~...~~ 2. ~~...~~ 3. An alien. 4. ~~...~~ 5. ~~...~~ }
(Strike out lines or words not applicable)

6 If not a citizen, of what Nation are you a citizen or subject? Italy

7 Father's birthplace Genoa (City or town) Italy (State or province) (Nation)

8 Name of employer Portland Railway Light & Power Co.
Place of employment (No.) (Street) Portland (City or town) Oregon (State)

9 Name of nearest relative George Rosi (Father)
Address of nearest relative (No.) (Street) Genoa (City or town) Italy (State or Nation)

10 Race White, ~~...~~
(Strike out words not applicable)

I affirm that I have verified above answers and that they are true.

Andrew Rosi
(Signature or Mark of Registrant)

P.M.G.O. Form 1 (blue)

REGISTRATION CARD.

Illus. 22. SELECTIVE SERVICE REGISTRATION CARD, SECOND CALL, JUNE 5, 1918

62

REGISTRATION CARD

SERIAL NUMBER 26-4

ORDER NUMBER 2928

1 Oscar John Johnson
First name — Middle name — Last name

2 PERMANENT HOME ADDRESS:
4926 Medill Ave Chicago Cook Illa
(No.) Street or R. F. D. No. — City — County — State

Age in Years 3 43

Date of Birth 4 Aug 22nd 1875

RACE

White	Negro	Oriental		Indian
			Citizen	Noncitizen
5 ✓	6	7	8	9

U. S. CITIZEN

Native Born 10 · Naturalized 11 · Citizen by Father's Naturalization Before Registrant's Majority 12 ·

ALIEN

Declarant · Non-declarant 14

13 ✓

15 If not a citizen of the U. S., of what nation are you a citizen or subject?
Sweden

PRESENT OCCUPATION · EMPLOYER'S NAME

16 Labor in Butterine Factory 17 John Johnke

18 PLACE OF EMPLOYMENT OR BUSINESS
Polk & Westernaw Chicago Cook Ills
(No.) Street or R. F. D. No. — City — County — State

NEAREST RELATIVE
19 Name Mrs Hanna Johnson
20 Address 4926 Medill Ave Chicago Cook Illl

I AFFIRM THAT I HAVE VERIFIED ABOVE ANSWERS AND THAT THEY ARE TRUE

P. M. G. O.
Form No. 1 Red.

Oscar Johnson

Illus. 23. SELECTIVE SERVICE REGISTRATION CARD, THIRD CALL, SEPTEMBER 12, 1918

Special Naturalization Actions

LAND PURCHASE

Indiana passed a law January 14, 1818, requiring any alien who purchased "lands, tenements and hereditaments within this state" to have made a declaration of intention. This law was replaced by one which, as an alternative to the declaration, stated that the alien "shall make an oath of affirmation in writing . . . to be recorded, that he is a resident of this state," and that he would "become a citizen . . . as soon as he can be naturalized" before becoming eligible to hold title to land. This oath required recording in the recorder's office where the land was located. The Act was repealed January 13, 1846, requiring from that time forward mere residence in the United States.[98]

In New York, beginning April 21, 1825, "any alien . . . may take and hold lands and real estate . . . . Provided, that no alien shall be capable of taking or holding any lands or real estate unless and until he shall have made a deposition or affirmation in writing, . . . that he is a resident in, and intends always to reside in the United States, and to become a citizen thereof as soon as he can be naturalized . . . that such deposition . . . shall be filed in the secretary's office of this state, and shall be recorded by the secretary of state, in a book or books to be by him kept for recording such depositions . . . ." His rights to own property expired six years after filing the deposition. This law, as amended, was repealed by a law effective April 1, 1913: "Alien friends are empowered to take, hold, transmit and dispose of real property within the state in the same manner as native-born citizens." The New York State Archives has 92 volumes of these petitions. Similar laws and additional recordings of intention may exist for other states.[99]

This requirement of filing a declaration of intention for land purchase was federalized under the Homestead Act, 1862. The thought of free land and large migration westward in the nineteenth century may force a conclusion that little was left for homesteading for aliens in the twentieth century. This is false. For the period thought to be most active for filing final homestead entries, 1868-1891,

400,345 were issued. In contrast to this twenty-nine year period, for the decade of 1913-1922, 399,528 final homestead entries were made. 1913 was a peak year with 53,252 filed. While I have not searched for any correlation, the period starting in 1905 corresponds to a large increase in the arrival of aliens. Genealogists should search homestead records. Generally, the National Archives has records prior to May 1, 1908, and the Bureau of Land Management after that date.[100]

Naturalization records document the resident alien's status for other activities, such as employment, passports, or licensing. The National Archives maintains records on federal employment and passport applications, which are discussed in *Guide to the Genealogical Records in the National Archives*.[101] States have required the filing of declarations of intention for professional licensing, and some government offices as well as the private sector have required proof of naturalization. Most of these latter records are of recent origin and generally are confidential. But by working from the obvious to the obscure, an elusive naturalization question may be solved if such secondary records provide a time and place where naturalization activity occurred.

NATIVE-BORN NATURALIZED WOMEN

On June 19, 1877, Hiram and Harriet Quick Anness became parents of a girl, Lula Pearl, born in Brookville Township, Franklin County, Indiana. On January 25, 1909, she married Charles Herrmann at Brookville. Although she lived nowhere else than Indiana she was naturalized an American citizen March 7, 1938. How is this possible? The Act of Congress passed March 2, 1907, section 3, stated: " . . . that any American woman who married a foreigner shall take the nationality of her husband." This section of the law was repealed by the Act of September 22, 1922, but it did not restore citizenship. From that date until June 25, 1936, a native-born American woman who married an alien had to file a petition for citizenship, provide proof and witnesses to the facts of her petition and character, and take an oath of allegiance to regain her citizenship and to receive a certificate of naturalization. As a result of the Act of June 25, 1936, she had to prove that she was a native-born American, that she lost her citizenship by marriage to a foreigner, and that the marriage had terminated. She was required to take only the oath of allegiance, using Form 2234, which stated the facts to be proved, one copy remaining in the court where naturalized and the other being filed with the naturalization service. While this 1907 law may not have affected many women, it requires investigation if an ancestor married an alien.[102]

Accessing the Records

WORK PROJECTS ADMINISTRATION NATURALIZATION PROJECT

With passage of the Alien Registration Act June 28, 1940, beginning August 27th, all aliens residing more than thirty days in the United States were required to register at local post offices, the latter forwarding the registry to the Immigration and Naturalization Service. "For the first time in the history of our nation, a complete inventory was to be made of all noncitizens."[103] However, prior to 1906, there were no centralized naturalization records of petitioners or those minors who derived citizenship from their parent. Nationalized records existed for only thirty-four years. Combining a labor force already at work in county courthouses with the need for efficient retrieval of evidence to document the citizenship of those who claimed to be naturalized under the "old law," the Department of Justice sponsored a nationwide project to locate and photocopy those records found in every court. Beginning in the fall of 1941, this short-lived project's purpose was to inventory and index each naturalization proceeding (intention, petition, and order of the court) found in separate naturalization ledgers, packets, or in the various books of official court proceedings. Upon completion of the inventory, a camera crew was to film or photocopy each record. These were to be deposited in Washington, D.C. The project, administered by the Work Projects Administration, included both federal and local trial courts.

There were varying degrees of completion. Both indexes and photocopies of pre-September, 1906, naturalization records found in Maine, Massachusetts, New Hampshire, Rhode Island, and Vermont, as well as those for New York City, were made and now are at NARA'S Northeast Region and also are on microfilm.[104] An index was completed and published for Philadelphia, 1789-1906.[105] Indexes for Alabama, Louisiana, Mississippi, Texas, Nebraska, and Iowa[106] were compiled, as well as one for parts of Illinois, Indiana, and Wisconsin. [107] Probably many states compare to Indiana. The initial phase of the project generated inventory sheets, which, after this work ended, were usually deposited in the

State Archives, as was the case in Indiana. The Indiana Historical Society organized these sheets into a single computerized index.[108] The entries, about 43,500, show name, county, and order book of the naturalization proceeding by volume and page. It is possible that other state archives may have similar records. In addition, the Historical Records Survey published a *Guide to Naturalization Records in Florida and a Guide to Naturalization Records in New Jersey*, 1941. The latter gives a good history of both colonial and early naturalization laws.

CENTRALIZATION OF NATURALIZATION RECORDS

Naturalization records are federal records and belong to the United States Government. Creation, custody, access, and disposal of these records remains under the authority of the Department of Justice. The Commissioner of Naturalization in his 1913 annual report said these courts "should properly be designed simply as naturalization courts." "With respect to their exercise of jurisdiction under the Act of June 29, 1906, they are all federal courts, since they equally operate under authority of a federal statute and confer a right authorized solely in the Constitution of the United States."[109] The Commissioner merely was restating a 1910 U.S. Supreme Court decision: "A state court which accepts naturalization jurisdiction performs this function as an agency of the federal government". [110] This position was restated as recently as 1997 in *Printz v. United States*. The U.S. Supreme Court noted that "these early laws establish, at most, that the Constitution was originally understood to permit imposition of an obligation on state *judges* to enforce federal prescriptions, insofar as those prescriptions related to matters appropriate for the judicial power.[111] The Indiana Court of Appeals observed, in 1913, that " . . . state courts in naturalization cases act as an agency of the federal government, and its officers are officers of the federal government in that behalf, and hence under the provisions of the Act of Congress".[112] On June 25, 1948, Congress passed a law restricting reproduction of naturalization and citizenship papers: "Whoever, without lawful authority, prints, photographs, makes or executes any print or impression of the likeness of a certificate of arrival, declaration of intention to become a citizen, or certificate of naturalization or citizenship, or any part thereof"[113] could be fined or imprisoned. The Immigration and Naturalization Service, in its manual dated December 5, 1972, distinguished between certified and uncertified copies and since that date has permitted the making of uncertified copies.[114] This "ownership" issue is important to researchers since the Department of Justice has permitted transfer of records from state and county level trial courts to state archives and federal regional archives. With the lifting of the prohibition to copy, the Genealogical Society of Utah, as well as many state archives, have microfilmed naturalization records and have made copies available to local libraries and courthouses.[115] *It is important to remember, however, that distinct naturalization records, kept separate from the regular proceedings and filings of the court, are the ones that are being centralized.*

# Research Procedures

enealogy, as stated in the beginning, can be simple. Frequently, it becomes quite difficult because the family historian tries to do too much at once. The best strategy is to divide and conquer. By breaking each element of a genealogical search into its lowest common denominator one can achieve the greatest success. Ask a series of questions about each of the five categories of information sought:

Name Look for as many variations of spelling as possible. See if nicknames were used rather than given names. Spell the name phonetically. Check census soundex lists to determine variations of name spellings that could sound the same to one who kept the records but was not familiar with the name. Determine how the immigrant ancestor spelled his or her name on official records, on birth certificates of children, on marriage licenses, and on deed and other land records.

Date Since many immigrants in the nineteenth century arrived near or after the age of 21, determine if he or she was able to sign legal documents in the United States, such as for the purchase of land. The 1900, 1910, and 1920 census records will tell how long the person lived in the United States. Examine church records, newspaper accounts and obituaries, and cemetery records for further clues to a date. Remember, it is important to estimate an ancestor's arrival in the United States as closely as possible to determine which naturalization law was applicable.

Place Early immigrants had to list former residences to prove that they were in the U.S. for five years. Since they usually settled near neighbors from the old country, or with relatives, and usually belonged to the same church, population movements by these groups could possibly provide clues to where an ancestor first settled and filed his or her declaration of intention.

Event By examining the major events in a person's life, including his or her education, political, social, and cultural activities, and by checking records kept by the associated organizations, additional information may be found to help locate an individual at the time when a naturalization event occurred.

Relationship The location of brothers and sisters, aunts and uncles, children, in-laws and other members of the family through similar searches of census records, ship passenger lists, church, and other records may offer suggestions that link your ancestor to when and where he or she filed their declaration of intention or petition for citizenship.

As stated in the beginning, one seeks five levels of information from three categories of records. Once this is done, one also is bound to examine the findings for accuracy and completeness. Apply an evaluation quiz to determine the quality and accuracy of the information.[116] It is critical to understand that naturalization records are **not** created for genealogical purposes, and the basic method of judicial record keeping, filing and recording, can lead to errors. Therefore, ask these questions:

(1) Is the information complete, a summary, or an abstract?

Court decisions frequently summarize the pleading but are complete in the judgment or decree. Indexes abstract data and reorganize it. Therefore, locate the appropriate record book *and* case file to obtain all the information.

(2) Is the data contemporary with the event?

The only contemporary data on a declaration or petition is the date of filing. Biographical information on the parties, such as birth dates, parents, and former marriages, occurred earlier, and that information may not be accurate.

(3) Is the record the official record of the office holder?

Is the record one that future legal decisions can be based upon? A clerk can certify almost anything, but the certificate states that "I certify that this as a true and compete copy of the original in my office." Certification does not make the pleading accurate. The decision, judgment, or decree of the court is its official record. Generally, an official record is one created by the clerk in performing his or her "official" function as opposed to records presented before that person.

(4) Is it the original or a copy?

To record is to copy. Ledger entries are copies of the original. Every time one copies something, it is subject to the copier's interpretation, be it a court official or a genealogist abstracting data. Is the handwriting contemporary with the time the record originally was created? How are spellings of names interpreted? The greater the passage of time from creation of the original to the date of the copy, the less scrutiny is given to the accuracy of the data. This may explain why a private record can be more accurate than a naturalization record, since the court document may be a copy, subject to errors, while the private one is an original. An alien, too, would be less likely to correct a clerk because of a spelling or name error since he or she probably would have been at least slightly intimidated.

(5) What is the reason one originally provided the information?

Was it for a benefit, like obtaining title to land? Was naturalization done at the behest of another, so the naturalization process was part of voter fraud and the information may be false? One can classify records as to accuracy based upon benefits sought.

(6) There is a corollary to the reason for giving information.

What penalty was there for guaranteeing the accuracy of the information? After September, 1906, if one gave false information on a naturalization record, he or she could be deported.

Quality courthouse records, then, are complete, contemporary with their creation, official, original, and given under penalty.

The critical element in locating records about a naturalization is resolved by researching descriptive records about courts. The federal statutes required "courts of records," that is, courts having among other elements, a permanent record of its proceedings. If the researcher relates this knowledge to the naturalization "record," one notes that there are *two types:*

(1) The naturalization record that is separate and distinct from all other proceedings of the court. Separate ledger books for naturalization became commonplace in the 1850's and under the Naturalization Act of 1906 were mandatory. When one consults the Family History Library Catalog of the LDS Family History Library, published lists of naturalization records, or the Internet, the ledgers are **all** one finds listed. It is important to remember the second class of records.

(2) Entries in the court's appropriate minute or order book, as well as original, loose papers or filings also exist. These usually remain with the court, even if "naturalization records," have been transferred to a state archives, or have been extracted. For periods before naturalization records were kept separately, or for courts which maintained no separate ledger series (and even those that did), one must also consult the regular court proceedings and files.

Illus. 24.
Order Book entry of the declaration of intention of James Hodge. (Clinton County, Indiana Circuit Court Civil Order Book 3, 93.)

Knowledge of the importance of naturalization courts being "courts of record," is meaningful also in locating any and all courts that naturalized within a county or state. The frustrated genealogist should use additional descriptive records about courts; namely, what courts naturalized, when, and did such jurisdiction overlap. It is critical to do the genealogy of the courts so one is not mislead by publications that fail to understand the distinction between separate naturalization records and filings and recordings in the citizenship process. One book described Indiana courts having naturalization records: "Naturalization records in Indiana can be found in county and U.S. district courts. Courts of common pleas processed all naturalization papers before 1813. Circuit courts also began handling these records after 1813. They stopped accepting naturalization in 1853 but began again in 1873. The state supreme court also processed naturalization from 1856 to 1906. The superior court took over the jurisdiction of naturalization cases in 1909. After 1930 district courts also processed naturalization."[117]

A researcher not familiar with Indiana's judicial history, potentially could fail to find Indiana's naturalization courts if he or she followed that list exclusively. Territorial Courts of Common Pleas ceased in 1813 and were replaced by Circuit Courts, many of which naturalized *continuously*, from 1814 until they relinquished their authority in the 1920's to the 1960's. A separate Court of Common Pleas, 1853-1873, *also* naturalized, along with the Circuit Court as did Superior Courts, the first of which were established in Indiana in 1872. Not mentioned are Indiana's Probate Courts, 1829-1852, which naturalized, especially after 1843. U.S. District Courts also naturalized prior to 1931.

Publications of lists of naturalization records, as well as this study, cannot fully describe the judicial history of each county in the United States; and if, or when, they might have exercised naturalization jurisdiction. However, there is a means for each researcher to do exactly that, for virtually every state or county he or she is researching. As part of a WPA project in the late 1930's and early 1940's, the federal government established an Historical Records Survey that published in excess of 600 inventories of county archives for forty-four of the then forty-eight states. In addition to listing separate naturalization records, each gave a history of the functions and jurisdiction of every court. Inventories for some county archives in each state are better than others. The best inventory for Indiana is the one for Tippecanoe County. WPA inventories for Mississippi refer to the one for Lamar County as having a full description of the history and functions of the courts. Likewise, other Tennessee inventories direct the researcher to Loudon County for complete histories of courts and their jurisdictions. Thus, by consulting an inventory for the state in which one is interested in understanding which courts performed naturalization, the researcher could find that all the courts during each's existence that could, and indeed which did, exercise its naturalization jurisdiction.

How does one find these publications? Everton's *Handy Book* [118] shows which counties had published an inventory of its county archives. It is vital to remember that one is not looking for references to naturalization records. One is seeking knowledge of which courts in a state naturalized, and when and where they did. Published with federal funding, these inventories are public documents and have been placed in depository libraries in each state, as well as in a number of public and special libraries.

Many state libraries offer interlibrary loan of these to local libraries, so if one were planning a trip from Kansas to Ohio, one could request the loan of an Ohio inventory before leaving and have the necessary knowledge to know which courts might have performed the naturalization process for that illusive immigrant ancestor.

For example, the WPA inventory for North Carolina notes:

"In a similar way the Clerks of Superior Court in North Carolina and the clerks of similar courts in other states are empowered to act as federal agents in the naturalization of aliens. Aliens' declarations of intention to become citizens and their petitions for naturalization may be filed with the Clerk of Superior Court and are occasionally to be found in his office . . . . As few aliens are naturalized in North Carolina, and at most aliens who do seek naturalization in the state address their petitions to the federal courts, this record is not often found and is almost never complete to date. Since 1927 each Clerk has been required to keep a register of all aliens over sixteen years of age resident in his county who have been or are to be in the state for more than ninety days. The register should include the name, nationality, date of birth, profession or occupation, present address, address before moving to state, and record of military service of each alien, together with the name and addresses of five person who know him. As there are few aliens in the state, however, the record is rarely kept."[119]

These suggestions must be tailored to family tradition but can assist in relating traditional records used by genealogists to specific problems in locating an immigrant ancestor. Because laws, procedures, and record keeping practices changed so many times before 1906, the greater detail you can provide in both time and place, the more successful your research can be [see Appendix V].

How should one proceed? Combine family knowledge with general information. From such sources as the 1820, 1830, and 1900-1920 censuses, regarding your ancestor's naturalization status, examine more specific records. Fit your ancestor in a time and place, and use information regarding citizenship laws in effect at that time. What procedures, if any, were followed, especially in the court's jurisdiction where he or she lived? From this information determine what forms were required, such as a registry, declaration of intention, certificate of arrival, petition, oath, depositions, and affidavits of witnesses, and certificates of naturalization. Consider also such special circumstances as military service, filing a homestead claim, obtaining a passport, and employment. Or, if it is suspected that an ancestor voted, remember that many states required only a declaration of intention to do so. When considering courts, work from the specific to the general, from a local court and its civil proceedings to other courts whose jurisdiction overlapped, to courts of statewide jurisdiction as a state supreme or a federal court. By knowing the laws, their exceptions and special handling of naturalization for those under special situations, and by knowing the procedures in effect to implement the law, you can make the naturalization system work for you.

To assist the family historian locate court records classified or grouped as "naturalization records," there are four broad categories of sources: (1) *Passenger and Immigration Lists Index,* (2) PERSI and published guides and lists to records, (3) the LDS Family History Library Catalog, and (4) the Internet. The first is an index to individual names while the latter three relate to listings of distinct naturalization records and holdings.

Passenger and Immigration Lists Index, with P. William Filby as chief editor, along with others, first appeared as a three volume work in 1981. It contains approximately 480,000 names from 300 sources. Beginning in 1982, and yearly thereafter, supplemental single volumes have appeared based upon new publications listing individuals. Phillip Hyde, whose naturalization declaration appears in Illus. 4, is listed in the 1982 Supplement, as "Hyde, Philip n. a. New York (state) 1830 2182 p. 60." The original source is a listing of Franklin County, Indiana, naturalization records that appeared in *The Hoosier Genealogist. An Index to Indiana Naturalization Records Found in Various Order Books of the Ninety-two Local Courts Prior to 1907*, published by the Indiana Historical Society, 1981, is indexed in the 1986 Supplement: "Hyde, Philip n. a. IN n.d. 3434 p. 74." This publication makes no distinction between immigration, ship passenger lists, naturalization, and other similar records; it is invaluable as a locator tool for individual names.

An excellent parallel publication to Filby's is the **PER**iodical Source Index, PERSI, published by the Allen County Public Library Foundation, Fort Wayne, Indiana. Begun in 1986 as a yearly compilation of articles on genealogical topics, it also has a retroactive series, 1847-1985. The complete set is now available on CD-Rom. References to naturalization records are found under several categories. If looking for references to naturalization records on the state level, one would check the state listing in the location field, for naturalization records pertaining only to that county, under the appropriate county, and finally, under "Research Methodology." For example, if one were interested in the holdings of a state archives this would be under the state heading. If one utilizes the PERSI listings fully, one is more successful. Persistence can pay off. This index will give the title of the article, the name of the journal, volume and issue number, and month and date of publication.[120]

There are many individual publications of naturalization listings and holdings. Representative is *Persons of Foreign Birth In Nineteenth Century Scott County, Indiana*, collected and compiled by Carl R. Bogardus and William R. Greear, Austin-Scottsburg, Indiana, 1969. In addition to listing individuals from separate naturalization books, it lists individuals of foreign birth from the census population schedules and naturalization proceedings found in the Order Books of the various Scott County Courts. An example of a listing of holdings is *How to Find Oregon Naturalization Records*, Connie Lenzen, Portland, revised March, 1989. In addition to listing territorial and federal naturalization records, and holdings for each of Oregon's 36 counties, it contains examples of naturalization documents. These are representative of many publications found in card catalogs, Filby, or PERSI.

The Genealogical Society of Utah has microfilmed a number of naturalization records in local courts throughout the United States. It is important to know, however, the date of microfilming to determine if all naturalization records in a county have been filmed. Until the early 1980's, the Society microfilmed citizenship ledgers dated prior to September 27, 1906. In 1984 it set policy to microfilm naturalization records through 1930, and in 1985 began microfilming records created by federal courts. The Society issues its "LDS Family History Library Catalog" both on microfiche and on CD-Rom. The last issuance, on CD-Rom, lists holdings catalogued as of March, 1997. It is important to note the distinction between *cataloging* and *microfilming*. The CD-Rom lists holdings *cataloged* as of March, 1997. Items cataloged also give the date of *microfilming*. Check the date of filming to see if the Society has naturalization records filmed prior to 1906 (that is, done prior to its change in policy in the early 1980's) or through 1930. It is quite possible that records exist on the county court or on the state court level that have not yet been microfilmed by the Society.

As an example, to determine the location of all naturalization records for Hancock County, Indiana, one would not consult the *Passenger and Immigrants Lists Index*, since this series lists individual names. *Locating Your Immigrant Ancestors*, (1986) states that the clerk's office has no pre-1906 naturalization records. If one consults the LDS Family History Library Catalog one finds "Naturalization Records, 1880-1906, Hancock County (Indiana), filmed in 1980. This is microfilm of the original records located at the Hancock County Courthouse, Greenfield, Indiana." This same data appears in the *Guide to Naturalization Records*. PERSI does not list naturalization record holdings under "Hancock County, Indiana," nor under "Research Methodology." If one uses the state heading, "Indiana," one finds a listing for " Naturalization records in the Indiana State Archives. *The Hoosier Genealogist*, March, 1993." Upon consulting this issue, one would find, among other county-court level naturalization records, those for Hancock County. The pre-1906 records, as well as later ones, were transferred to the Indiana State Archives in 1982.

The researcher should also check the catalog to see if the Society microfilmed probate or civil proceedings (minute or order books). For example, in addition to having microfilmed individual naturalization ledgers for a number of Ohio Probate Courts, the Genealogical Society of Utah has filmed their Probate Journals and Chancery Records. They have done the same for the Indiana Probate Courts' Order Books, 1829 - 1852. Among settlements of estates one frequently find naturalization records.

The Internet has the potential to be the universe of locator records about naturalization. The amount of genealogical information on line boggles one's mind. The Internet offers the researcher the capability for having the most current information, replacing published lists, as well as data provided by those most knowledgeable about the records. On the other hand, there are no criteria for evaluating the quality of the information. One should seek three broad web sites when attempting to locate information about naturalization and to locate the records themselves: (1) the National Archives; (2) State Archives (all but Nebraska currently have Web pages) and (3) genealogical Web pages [See Appendix III for Web site addresses]. New York's State Archives and Records Administration has an excellent "Guide to Naturalization Records" and the Indiana State Archives has begun to list individual names on line. Among the more useful sites is the USGenWeb project,[121] whose resources generally are arranged through access to counties. Begun in June, 1996, in Kentucky, it has spread throughout the United States and beyond. One has the potential for locating citizenship information under "Naturalization" headings, under individual states, and for individual counties. Local volunteers sponsor a home page and share their knowledge not only about record holdings but also with tips on how to use them. In addition to finding a listing of naturalization holdings for Erie County (Buffalo), New York, one finds the following caution: "The indexes appear to be full of spelling errors and omissions, and some researchers have not been replacing the cards back in alphabetical order, so be sure to check backwards and forwards from where your ancestor should be and all alternative spellings."[122] Information on the Internet, as with all secondary sources, should be considered descriptive and locator material, and not identifier data. All resources must be checked for relevance, accuracy, and completeness.

For original citizenship records after the 1906 date, it is better to first contact the local court or if the records have been centralized, the state archives. One then can file a Freedom of Information Act/Privacy Act Request, Form G-639 (amended September 11, 1996) with the Immigration and Naturalization Service. For files from September 27, 1906 through March 31, 1956, write to the Service at 425 I Street NW, Washington, DC 20536. For records beginning April 1, 1956, write to the appropriate office where the alien lived.[123] Given the Freedom of Information Act requirements and greater difficulty of access, one should attempt to locate naturalization records after September 27, 1906, in the appropriate federal regional archives, state archives, and courthouses. Combine knowledge about procedure with knowledge about record depositories.

Pointers

- Develop a time and place sequence for the immigrant ancestor.

- Determine what naturalization laws were in effect at the time (see Appendix I and text, pages 13-20)

- Was there a requirement that compelled an ancestor to file a declaration, or become naturalized, as

  - voting rights (page 50)

  - World War I draft registration (pages 58-60)

  - land purchase (pages 65-66)

- Assume that no record keeping standards existed before September 27, 1906.

- Seek both separate naturalization records and the regularly filed court records, which remain in case files or permanent ledger books within the court.

- Determine what courts, when, could, or did naturalize and see if jurisdictions overlapped. (See WPA pages 67-68)

- It generally is easier to find post September 27, 1906, naturalization records on the county or state level than to go through the Immigration and Naturalization Service.

- Use the Internet as the most current tool for locating separately maintained naturalization records by consulting the National Archives, state archives, and county web sites.

- Remember that the original declaration of intention was kept by the clerk of the court with a copy given to the individual who had to surrender it when filing a petition. This means:

  - If you have a manuscript declaration among personal papers, it strongly suggests that an ancestor never petitioned for citizenship; and

- Loss of naturalization records due to a courthouse fire may be offset by the recording of the declaration in a different county, or in a federal court, when the person moved to another county or state and petitioned for citizenship.

- Read the introduction to any publication consulted, and use their references as a tool for additional research. [This is why there is so much detail and so many notes in this publication: what I consider unimportant may be the exact source you need to make the connection.]

Do not be discouraged. Too many writers and speakers have commented that "naturalization records created prior to 1906 contain little of genealogical value"; or, "prior to 1906, naturalization proceedings could take place in any court of law--city, county, district, state, or federal. After that date, this process was confined to the federal courts."[124] The purpose here is not to criticize such writers; the recommendation is to question all absolute statements since they may be based on facts not in evidence. If one seeks a name, date, place, and naturalization event, any citizenship record can have value. If one understands the genealogy of the creation of naturalization records, additional documents or entries can provide an arrival date, port of entry, age or birth date, or places of residence before a "naturalization record of little value" becomes the only record located without any additional searching. Trust in yourself, based upon as much knowledge as possible, rather than judgmental generalities.

"History is the distillation of evidence surviving from the past."
Oscar Handlin *Truth in History*

The genealogist, like the historian, seeks the truth. "Truth," Handlin writes, "resides in the small pieces which together form the record."[125] For naturalization research, virtually all evidence is in the form of public records. Research must be based upon knowledge. By knowing the genealogy of the naturalization process and the resulting records, one adds another tool to one's methodology for locating immigrant ancestors and their naturalization records. Knowledge about naturalization records, and the where and when, has been the purpose of this book. The general literature discusses what was supposed to have happened; this book attempts to provide a planning strategy to determine what probably did occur, both in record creation and in procedure. If the record does not seem to exist on first glance, a family tradition of naturalization may still be true after all; but given the tools discussed here, the family historian may have greater success upon additional searching.

Knowledge reduces uncertainty.

I Naturalization Processes by Person and Time

The following list of procedures for naturalization is arranged by person, function, date, and comment. It provides an overview of basic naturalization requirements to assist the genealogist establish time frames for an ancestor. This list is general in nature and does not purport to detail all laws, amendments, and supplements nor changes brought about by promulgation of rules. Consult laws for specific language and function regarding citizenship. Generally last dates end with the act of October 14, 1940, effective January 13, 1941, unless requirements began at that time. For later status of laws governing these functions, see the act of June 27, 1952, as amended, and the act of November 29, 1990, as amended, 8 U.S.C.A.

PETITIONER

1. REGISTRY

6/18/1798-5/24/1828	Aliens residing in U.S. shall report themselves for registry.
3/22/1816-5/24/1828	Report and declaration had to be filed with court before granting citizenship.
5/26/1824	Any naturalization certificate issued not in conformity with act of 3/22/1816 is valid.
6/29/1911-current	Alien immigrants to be registered and certificate of arrival issued. Certificate to be attached to petition for naturalization. Affects arrivals of aliens after 6/29/1906.
7/01/1929-8/06/1939	Certificate of arrival waived if no record found, alien entered U.S. prior to 6/03/1921, and had resided in the U.S. continuously. Certificate of arrival filed with declaration of intention. Temporary one year amendment made under act of 6/08/1934 regarding aliens who were not deportable and who arrived prior to 7/01/1933 with no proof of arrival.
8/07/1939-12/23/1952	Same provisions as above for alien who arrived prior to 7/01/1924.

2. DECLARATION OF INTENTION

<u>GENERAL</u>

3/26/1790-1/28/1795	None required.
1/29/1795-6/17/1798	Required if naturalized after 4/14/1802; none required if naturalized prior to 4/14/1804.
6/18/1798-4/13/1802	Required; if naturalized after 3/2``6/1804 none required.
4/14/1802-6/11/1812	Required; if naturalized after 5/24/1828 none required.
6/12/1812- 12/23/1952	Required.
12/24/1952-current	Discretionary.

<u>FORMS</u>

1/29/1795-9/26/1906	None used or a variety of types and formats.
9/27/1906-6/30/1929	Form 2202.
7/01/1929-1/12/1941	Form 2202 L-A.
1/13/1941-current	Form N-315.

<u>EXEMPTIONS</u>

See Aliens Misinformed as to Citizenship; Military; Spouses; Children.

3. PETITION FOR NATURALIZATION

3/26/1790-current	Required. Early acts referred to it as "application."
6/01/1903-9/26/1906	Special form used to meet language regarding anarchists in 1903 act. Frequently separate ledgers created.

<u>FORMS</u>

3/26/1790-9/26/1906	Entered into the proceedings of the court. By late 1840's some courts had ledgers for "Second Papers" or "Final Record." Nature of form and format varied greatly.
9/27/1906-6/30/1929	Form 2204.
7/01/1929-1/12/1941	Form 2204 L-A.
1/13/1941-current	Form N-405.

4. CERTIFICATE OF NATURALIZATION

GENERAL

3/26/1790-9/26/1906	Part of the official proceedings of the court; entered into appropriate order or minute book. At any time a separate certificate could be issued to naturalized petitioner.
9/27/1906-current	Recorded in separate ledger books or after ca. 1925 on loose sheets. Original order of citizenship entered in Petition Record; original certificate issued to petitioner; duplicate sent to Naturalization Service and the stub, later a 3" x 5" card, retained by the court.

FORMS

3/26/1790-9/26/1906	Varies; no official form. Entry in proceedings for legal record.
9/27/1906-1/12/1941	Form 2207; stub (after ca. 1913, Form 390.)
1/13/1941-current	Form N-550.

5. RESIDENCE

3/26/1790-6/17/1798	Five years in U.S., one in state; 1/29/1795, residence proved by oath.
6/18/1798-4/13/1802	Fourteen years in U.S., five in state; if alien made declaration prior to 1/291795 he or she needed five years in U.S., if he or she made petition by 6/18/1799.
4/14/1802-current	Five years in U.S., one in state (changed to six months 10/14/1940); can't prove residence by oath, other proof required.
3/03/1813-current	Residence continuous. Cannot leave U.S. at any time (clause repealed 6/26/1848).
3/22/1816-current	Residence proved by oath of witnesses who must be U.S. citizens; five years' residence. Place or places of alien's residence stated in petition (repealed 9/27/1906).
5/24/1828-9/26/1906	If naturalized after 5/24/1828 based on residence from 4/14/1802 to 6/18/1812, must comply with residence requirement of 3/22/1816 act.
7/01/1929-current	No declaration filed until entry for permanent residence established; residence in county six months, exemption to residing continuously in U.S. (Act of 10/14/1940 changed residence from "county" to "state" but still six months.)
6/25/1936-1/12/1941	If alien works for U.S. government or business, does not affect continuous residency clause. (Conditions clarified by amendment of 6/29/1938).
8/09/1939-current	Residence exemption extended to clergy.

<u>EXEMPTIONS</u>

See military, spouse, children; see also Registry.

6. WITNESSES

3/26/1790-3/21/1816	None specified, but alien must prove to satisfaction of court residence of five years and good moral character.
3/22/1816-9/26/1906	Names of witnesses, U.S. citizens, who on oath swear to alien's five year residence in U.S., entered by name in record of court admitting alien.
6/01/1903-9/26/1906	Witnesses required to testify by affidavit that alien petitioner not an anarchist.
9/27/1906-current	Affidavits of two credible witnesses, U.S. citizens, as to residence and character, on form 2218, to accompany petition for naturalization. Their name, residence, and occupation set forth in record.
9/27/1906-current	Depositions of witnesses if alien not resident for five years where he or she filed petition. Same criteria as for affidavits.

7. NAME CHANGE

9/27/1906-current	At court hearing on naturalization, upon petition, may issue decree changing alien's name. New name to appear on certificate of naturalization.

8. ENEMY ALIENS

3/26/1790-5/08/1918	With certain exceptions no alien proscribed by any state, or convicted of having joined army of Great Britain during Revolutionary War, was permitted citizenship.
7/30/1813-5/08/1918	If alien filed declaration prior to 6/18/1812, he or she could become a citizen, not withstanding his or her status as enemy alien (War of 1812).
5/09/1918-current	No enemy alien permitted citizenship unless he or she made declaration not less than two years nor more than seven years prior to existence of state of war. President, upon recommendation of Department of Labor/Justice, can accept such alien from alien status. Enemy alien status existed only during periods of war.

9. PERSONS MISINFORMED AS TO CITIZENSHIP STATUS

6/25/1910-5/08/1918	If lived five years in U.S., continuously prior to 5/01/1910, no prior declaration of intention required.

5/09/1918-5/24/1932	If lived five years in U.S. continuously prior to 7/01/1914, and not an alien enemy, no prior declaration required.
5/25/1932-12/23/1952	Date changed to 7/01/1920. Act of 6/27/1952, effective 12/24/1952, repealed this law.

10. *ARMED FORCES*

MILITARY SERVICE

ENLISTMENTS

5/09/1918-current	WWI aliens in armed forces not required to file declaration or meet residency requirement nor have certificate of arrival and could be naturalized at military camps and nearby courts. Extended by acts of 7/19/1919, 5/26/1926, 3/04/1929, 5/25/1932, 6/24/1935 (two acts), 8/23/1937, 6/21/1939, and 10/14/1940. Later laws extended provision to WWII and later military actions.
8/01/1894-current	Enlistee in army has to be a U.S. citizen or had to have filed declaration, but act applied only during time of peace. Special suspension for Korean Conflict, Vietnam, and Desert Storm.

VETERANS

ARMY

7/17/1862-5/08/1918	Honorably discharged veterans from army could be naturalized with no filing of declaration and one year's residence. After 5/09/1918, this benefit was restricted to those who were discharged prior to 1/01/1900.

NAVY, MARINES

7/26/1894-5/08/1918	Same benefit afforded army veterans was extended to Navy and Marine personnel.
5/09/1918-current	The residency requirement for honorably discharged veterans of all services (Coast Guard added 7/30/1937) eliminated, but a declaration of intention required.

MERCHANT MARINES

6/07/1872-9/12/1935	Act of 6/07/1872, modified 5/09/1918, repealed 9/13/1935.
1/13/1941-current	Reenacted 10/14/1940 permitted naturalization of those who served in the U.S. Merchant Marines and who had filed a declaration previous to service without meeting residency requirement if honorably discharged.

SPOUSE

1. MARRIED WOMAN

3/26/1790-2/09/1855	No specific language in law covering derivative citizenship of wife of naturalized husband.
2/10/1855-9/21/1922	Any woman eligible for citizenship, who is or shall be married to a citizen of the U.S. shall be a citizen.
3/02/1907-9/21/1922	Any foreign woman who acquired U.S. citizenship by marriage shall retain same after termination of marriage if she continued to reside in U.S. or if living abroad she registered within one year.
9/22/1922-1/12/1941	An alien woman who marries an American does not become naturalized upon marriage. She must follow requirements of naturalization law except: no declaration of intention required; one year residency required.
5/24/1934-1/12/1941	Law amended to include man who married an American does not become naturalized by marriage. Also three years, not one year residency required.
1/13/1941-current	Act of 10/14/1940, secs. 310, 311, 312, and Act of 6/17/1952, have similar sections dealing with naturalization of alien women and spouses.

2. WIDOWS

3/26/1804-9/25/1906	Became citizen if husband had filed declaration and died before becoming naturalized upon her taking oath of allegiance.
9/26/1906-5/24/1934	Became citizen if husband had filed declaration and died before becoming naturalized if she complied with other provisions of law except filing a declaration.

3. WIFE OF INSANE PETITIONER

2/24/1911-5/23/1934	If alien became insane after filing declaration but before naturalization, wife, if she filed a homestead entry, may be naturalized without filing a declaration.

4. CERTIFICATE OF DERIVATIVE NATURALIZATION

7/01/1929-current	Spouse may receive certificate, upon application, under act of 3/02/1929 (permissive).

5. AMERICAN WOMEN

3/02/1907-9/21/1922	She who marries a foreigner shall take the nationality of her husband. At termination of marriage she must register within one year if living abroad or if living in U.S. by residing therein.
9/22/1922-current	Shall not lose citizenship upon marriage to an alien.
9/22/1922-6/24/1936	She who lost citizenship may become a citizen by following: no declaration, no certificate of arrival, and no period of residency required; compliance with general naturalization laws. Act of 5/24/1934 added husbands as well as wives. It also raised residency requirement to three years.
9/22/1922-3/03/1931	If husband not eligible for citizenship, could not be naturalized during marital status.
6/25/1936-current	She who lost citizenship by marriage to an alien prior to 9/22/1922 and whose marriage had terminated now required only to take oath of allegiance. 7/02/1940 act amended to add "or who has resided continuously" in U.S.

CHILDREN

1. ALIEN CHILDREN

3/26/1790-1/28/1795	Became citizen when parent naturalized.
1/29/1795-c`urrent	Becomes citizen when parent naturalized and if child is dwelling in U.S.
3/02/1907-5/23/1934	Citizenship began when child started to reside in U.S.
5/24/1934-current	Citizenship begins five years after minor child begins to reside in U.S.
3/26/1804-9/26/1906	Became citizen if father filed declaration and died before becoming naturalized upon child's taking oath of allegiance.

2. EXEMPTION FROM FILING DECLARATION OF INTENTION

3/26/1790-current	Generally no declaration required under acts of 1790, 1795, 1802, 1906, and 1940 if parent naturalized while child still a minor. Declaration discretionary after 12/24/1952.
5/26/1824-9/26/1906	Alien minor under age 21 who is resident of U.S. three years before age 21 and whose residence was continuous could make application for citizenship after arrival of age 21 and a total of five years residence: no previous declaration; must file declaration at time of admission.
9/27/1906-5/23/1934	If alien died after making declaration, but not yet naturalized, children are citizens by conforming with other naturalization proceedings without filing declaration.

2/24/1911-5/23/1934	Children of alien who had filed declaration then became insane and whose mother filed homestead entry could be naturalized without filing declaration if other provisions of act were met.
7/02/1940-12/23/1952	Any alien entering U.S. under 16 years, at age 21, could be naturalized with compliance to naturalization laws, except: no declaration required; petition for naturalization filed within one year of age 21.

3. *CERTIFICATE OF DERIVATIVE NATURALIZATION*

7/1/1929-current	Certificate is permissive under act of 3/02/1929 and later.

4. *ADOPTED CHILD*

1/13/1941-10/04/1978	Could be naturalized before age 18 upon petition of adoptive parent if child resided continuously for two years immediately before filing petition. Child and parents must be lawfully admitted to U.S., child adopted in U.S. before age sixteen and in legal custody of parents for two years.

5. *ILLEGITIMATE CHILD*

varies	A. If father declares paternity while child still a minor condition of alien child or child of U.S. citizen apply, based on nature of citizenship of father. Secretary of State traditionally applied this policy; sustained by opinion of U.S. Attorney General 4/07/1920 (32 OP. Atty. Gen. 162). Formalized by Act of 10/14/1940, sec. 204, effective 1/13/1941.
1/13/1941-current	B. In absence of such legitimation or adjudication, if mother is U.S. citizen and previously resided in U.S. then child acquires at birth her nationality status.

6. *STEP-CHILDREN*

2/10/1855-9/21/1922	Children of a wife by a former marriage acquired citizenship (or earlier) status through her second marriage upon the wife's second husband's naturalization. From 9/27/1906 through 9/21/1922, data on these step-children were listed on the petition and certificate of naturalization.

7. *CITIZENS AT BIRTH BORN ABROAD*

3/26/1790-current	These are U.S. Citizens. Their right of citizenship shall not descend to persons whose fathers never resided in U.S.

3/02/1907-5/23/1934	If they continued to reside outside of U.S., at age 18 they had to record their intention to become residents and remain U.S. citizens. At age 21 they had to take oath of allegiance.
5/24/1934-1/12/1941	But citizenship does not descend to child unless citizen parent had resided in U.S. previous to birth of said child, if one parent was an alien, citizenship does not descend unless child came to U.S. and resided therein for five years continuously previous to child's 18th birthday and unless within six months of child's 21st birthday he or she took oath of allegiance.
1/13/1941-current	If both parents are citizens and one has resided in U.S. prior to birth of said person.
1/13/1941-current	If one parent, prior to birth of such child, has 10 years' residence in U.S., five of which parent has had after age 16 and other parent is an alien, or child to retain such citizenship, he or she must reside in U.S. for five years between ages 13 and 21. This also applies to all children born abroad after 5/24/1934.
7/31/1941-current	Provisions apply to child if one parent served in WWII in armed forces rather than being a citizen.

Appendix II Census Records—Questions Relating to Foreign-born and Citizenship

Note that those living in the United States in 1789 when the U.S. Constitution was adopted were citizens and would not appear as foreigners not naturalized in the 1820 and 1830 censuses.

Census	Date	Data Field/Census taker's directions
1820	8/07/1820	"Foreigners not naturalized"
1830	6/01/1830	"ALIENS--Foreigners not naturalized"
1850	6/01/1850	No question regarding citizenship, but first to ask birthplace: Heading 9-- "insert . . . the name of the government or country if without the United States."
1860	6/01/1860	No question regarding citizenship but does ask for birthplace: Heading 10— "insert . . . the name of the government or country if without the United States."
1870	6/01/1870	Column 10 "Place of Birth naming . . . the Country, if of foreign birth." The instructions to the assistant marshals include: "Column 10 will contain the 'Place of birth' of every person named upon the schedule . . . . If of foreign birth, the country will be named as specifically as possible. Instead of writing 'Great Britain' as the place of birth, give the particular country, as England, Scotland, Wales. Instead of 'Germany,' specify the State, as Prussia, Baden, Bavaria, Wurttemburg, Hesse Darmstadt, etc." Column 11 asked if "father of foreign birth," and Column 12 asked if "mother of foreign birth." Columns 19 and 20 involved "Constitutional Relations." The instructions included this comment: "All persons born out of the limits and jurisdiction of the United States, whose fathers at the time of their birth were citizens of the United States (act of February 10, 1855); also, all persons born out of the limits and jurisdiction of the United States, who have been declared by judgment of court to have been duly naturalized, having taken out *both* "papers."

1880	6/01/1880	No questions regarding citizenship, but the 1880 census is the first to ask for the country if of foreign birth for the person, his/her father and his/her mother. The instructions for "place of birth" were similar to the instructions for the 1870 census.

1890   6/01/1890   [Note: Little of the 1890 Census survives.] Questions 10, 11, and 12 asked for birthplace of person, father, and mother. Questions 13, 14, and 15 inquired as to citizenship: 13--"Number of years in the United States"; 14--"Whether naturalized"; 15--"Whether naturalization papers have been taken out." The instructions to enumerators regarding birthplaces generally followed the instructions for place of birth found in the 1870 census but specified "country" and not "city." In addition it inquired of those born abroad of American citizens. For Naturalization: "Inquiries 13, 14, and 15 should be made concerning only those adult *males* of foreign birth who are 21 years of age or over. *13. Number of years in the United States.* Give the answer in figures, as 1, 2, 3, 6 ,10, etc., according to the number of years such person (as stated above) may have resided in the United States. *14. Whether naturalized.* Write "*Yes*" or "*No*," as the case may be. *15. Whether naturalization papers have been taken out.* If naturalized (Inquiry 14), use the symbol X; if not naturalized (Inquiry 14), write "*Yes*" or "*No*," as the case may be, in answer to this inquiry (15).

1900   6/01/1900   "Nativity" Column 13. Direction 139: "If the person was born outside the United States, enter in column 13 the country (not city or district) in which he or she was born. By country is meant usually a region whose people have direct relation with other countries. Thus, do not write Prussia or Saxony, but Germany. To this rule, however, note the following exceptions: [140.] Write Ireland, England, Scotland, or Wales rather than Great Britain. Write Hungary or Bohemia rather than Austria for persons born in Hungary or Bohemia, respectively. **Write Finland rather than Russia for persons born in Finland.** "Citizenship" Columns 16, 17, 18: Direction 148: Column 16. **Year of immigration to the United States.**—If the person is a native of the United States, leave the column blank. If he or she was born abroad, enter the year in which he or she arrived in the United States. Direction 149: Column 17. **Number of years in the United States.**—If the person was born abroad, enter the number of years since his or her arrival in the United States. Disregard all fractions of a year. If the time is less than one year, write "**0.**" Endeavor to get the exact number of years in all cases. Direction 151. **Column 18. Naturalization.**—If the person was born abroad, and has taken no steps toward becoming an American citizen, write "**Al**" (for alien). If he has declared his intention to become an American citizen and taken out his "first" papers, write "**Pa**" (for papers). If he has become a full citizen by taking out second or final papers of naturalization, write "**Na**" (for naturalized). Direction 152. **The question of naturalization (column 18) applies only to foreign-born males 21 years of age and over. It does not apply to foreign-born minors, to foreign-born females, or to any person, male or female, who was born in the United States, either of native or foreign parentage.**

1910   4/15/1910   **131. Column 15. Year of immigration to the United States.**—This question applies to all foreign-born persons, male and female, of whatever age. It should be answered, therefore, for every person whose birthplace as reported in column 12 was in a foreign country. Enter the year in which the person came to the United States. If he or she has been in the United States more than once, give the year of the first arrival. **132. Column 16. Whether naturalized or alien.**—This question applies only to foreign-born males 21 years of age and over. It does not apply to females, to foreign-born minors, or to any male born in the United States. If the person was born abroad, but has become a full citizen, either by taking out second or final papers of naturalization or through the naturalization of his parents while he was under the age of 21 years, write "Na" (for naturalized). If he has declared his intention to become an American citizen and has taken out his "first papers," write "Pa" (for papers). If he has taken no steps toward becoming an American citizen, write "Al" (for alien).

1920	1/01/1920	The instructions were substantially the same as for 1910.
1930	4/01/1930	[Note: The 1930 Census is scheduled for release in 2002.] Columns 22, 23, and 24 relate to citizenship. **178. Column 22. Year of immigration to the United States.**—(See question # 131 for the 1910 census.) **179. Column 23. Naturalization.**—This question applies to all foreign-born persons, male and female, of whatever age. Prior to September 22, 1922, a foreign-born woman became a citizen when her husband was naturalized. Since that date, she must take out papers in her own name; and if she does not do this, she remains an alien even though her husband becomes naturalized. The question should be answered, therefore, for every person whose birthplace was in a foreign country, as follows: **180.** For a foreign-born male 21 years of age and over write "Na" (for "naturalized") if he has either (1) taken out second or final naturalization papers, or (2) become naturalized while under the age of 21 by the naturalization of either parent. **181.** For a foreign-born female 21 years of age and over write "Na" if she has either (1) taken out final papers, or (2) become naturalized through the naturalization of either parent while she was under the age of 21, or (3) if she became naturalized prior to 1922 by the naturalization of her husband. (See par. 179.) **182.** For a foreign-born person under 21 years of age write "Na" if either parent has been naturalized. This applies to infants and young children as well as to older persons under 21. **183.** For all foreign-born persons who have not been naturalized but have taken out first papers write "Pa" (for "papers"). Note that a person must be at least 18 years of age in order to take out first papers. Minor children should not be returned "Pa" merely because their parents have taken out first papers. **184.** For all foreign-born persons neither naturalized nor having first papers, write "Al" (for "alien").

Federal census data also provides information on the number of immigrants by nationality for each census year and the number of those naturalized by nationality, both by length of time in the United States and by each state. The following tables and charts may assist the researcher define when and where an ancestor of a certain nationality settled and the general likelihood of being naturalized based upon a statistical probability of the percentage of all those from that nationality who did. Unfortunately, these tables do not list those who were "subject of," rather than a citizen of, a country, since the former tended to be more motivated to seek citizenship.

TABLE 1. IMMIGRATION TO THE UNITED STATES:
1820 – 1956

From 1820 to 1867 figures represent alien passengers arrived; 1868 to 1891 inclusive and 1895 to 1897 inclusive immigrant aliens arrived; 1892 to 1894 inclusive and from 1898 to the present time immigrant aliens admitted.

Year	Number of persons	Year	Number of persons	Year	Number of persons	Year	Number of persons
1820-1956(1)	40,734,745	1851-1860	2,598,214	1884..	518,592	1921-1930	4,107,209
				1885..	395,346		
1820	8,385	1851..	379,466	1886..	334,203	1921..	805,228
		1852..	371,603	1887..	490,109	1922..	309,556
1821-1830	143,439	1853..	368,645	1888..	546,889	1923..	522,919
		1854..	427,833	1889..	444,427	1924..	706,896
1821..	9,127	1855..	200,877	1890..	455,302	1925..	294,314
1822..	6,911	1856..	200,436			1926..	304,488
1823..	6,354	1857..	251,306	1891-1900	3,687,564	1927..	335,175
1824..	7,912	1858..	123,126			1928..	307,255
1825..	10,199	1859..	121,282	1891..	560,319	1929..	279,678
1826..	10,837	1860..	153,640	1892..	579,663	1930..	241,700
1827..	18,875			1893..	439,730		
1828..	27,382	1861-1870	2,314,824	1894..	285,631	1931-1940	528,431
1829..	22,520			1895..	258,536		
1830..	23,322	1861..	91,918	1896..	343,267	1931..	97,139
		1862..	91,985	1897..	230,832	1932..	35,576
1831-1840	599,125	1863..	176,282	1898..	229,299	1933..	23,068
		1864..	193,418	1899..	311,715	1934..	29,470
1831..	22,633	1865..	248,120	1900..	448,572	1935..	34,956
1832..	60,482	1866..	318,568			1936..	36,329
1833..	58,640	1867..	315,722	1901-1910	8,795,386	1937..	50,244
1834..	65,365	1868..	138,840			1938..	67,895
1835..	45,374	1869..	352,768	1901..	487,918	1939..	82,998
1836..	76,242	1870..	387,203	1902..	648,743	1940..	70,756
1837..	79,340			1903..	857,046		
1838..	38,914	1871-1880	2,812,191	1904..	812,870	1941-1950	1,035,039
1839..	68,069			1905..	1,026,499		
1840..	84,066	1871..	321,350	1906..	1,100,735	1941..	51,776
		1872..	404,806	1907..	1,285,349	1942..	28,781
1841-1850	1,713,251	1873..	459,803	1908..	782,870	1943..	23,725
		1874..	313,339	1909..	751,786	1944..	28,551
1841..	80,289	1875..	227,498	1910..	1,041,570	1945..	38,119
1842..	104,565	1876..	169,986			1946..	108,721
1843..	52,496	1877..	141,857	1911-1920	5,735,811	1947..	147,292
1844..	78,615	1878..	138,469			1948..	170,570
1845..	114,371	1879..	177,826	1911..	878,587	1949..	188,317
1846..	154,416	1880..	457,257	1912..	838,172	1950..	249,187
1847..	234,968			1913..	1,197,892		
1848..	226,527	1881-1890	5,246,613	1914..	1,218,480	1951..	205,717
1849..	297,024			1915..	326,700	1952..	265,520
1850..	369,980	1881..	669,431	1916..	298,826	1953..	170,434
		1882..	788,992	1917..	295,403	1954..	208,177
		1883..	603,322	1918..	110,618	1955..	237,790
				1919..	141,132	1956..	321,625
				1920..	430,001		

(1) Data are for fiscal years ended June 30, except 1820 to 1831 inclusive and 1844 to 1849 inclusive fiscal years ended Sept. 30; 1833 to 1842 inclusive and 1851 to 1867 inclusive years ended Dec. 31; 1832 covers 15 months ended Dec. 31; 1843 nine months ended Sept. 30; 1850 fifteen months ended Dec. 31; and 1868 six months ended June 30.

TABLE 1: IMMIGRATION TO THE UNITED STATES, 1820 - 1956
(Report of the Immigration and Naturalization Service, 1956, 29)

FOREIGN-BORN POPULATION, BY COUNTRY OF BIRTH: 1860–1910.

Table 2

COUNTRY OF BIRTH.	FOREIGN-BORN POPULATION.						PER CENT OF TOTAL FOREIGN BORN.					
	1910	1900	1890	1880	1870	1860	1910	1900	1890	1880	1870	1860
All foreign countries	13,515,886	10,341,276	9,249,560	6,679,943	5,567,229	4,188,058	100.0	100.0	100.0	100.0	100.0	100.0
Austria	1,174,973	491,295	241,377	124,024	70,797	25,061	8.7	4.8	2.6	1.9	1.3	0.6
Belgium	49,400	29,757	22,639	15,535	12,553	9,072	0.4	0.3	0.2	0.2	0.2	0.2
Canada—French [2]	385,083	395,126	302,496	{717,157	493,464	249,970	2.8	3.8	3.3	{10.7	8.9	6.0
Canada—Other [1]	819,554	784,796	678,442	}			6.1	7.6	7.3	}		
China	56,756	81,634	106,701	104,468	63,042	35,565	0.4	0.8	1.2	1.6	1.1	0.8
Cuba and other West Indies	[3]47,635	[3]25,435	23,256	16,401	11,570	7,353	0.4	0.2	0.3	0.2	0.2	0.2
Denmark	181,649	153,690	132,543	64,196	30,107	9,962	1.3	1.5	1.4	1.0	0.5	0.2
England	877,719	840,513	909,092	664,160	555,046	433,494	6.5	8.1	9.8	9.9	10.0	10.4
France	117,418	104,197	113,174	106,971	116,402	109,870	0.9	1.0	1.0	1.6	2.1	2.6
Germany [1]	2,501,333	2,813,628	2,784,894	1,966,742	1,690,533	1,276,075	18.5	27.2	30.1	29.4	30.4	30.5
Greece	101,282	8,515	1,887	776	390	328	0.7	0.1	(4)	(4)	0.1	(4)
Hungary	495,609	145,714	62,435	11,526	3,737		3.7	1.4	0.7	0.2	(4)	
Ireland	1,352,251	1,615,459	1,871,509	1,854,571	1,855,827	1,611,304	10.0	15.6	20.2	27.8	33.3	38.5
Italy	1,343,125	484,027	182,580	44,230	17,157	11,677	9.9	4.7	2.0	0.7	0.3	0.3
Japan	67,744	24,788	2,292	401	73		0.5	0.2	(4)	(4)	(4)	
Mexico	221,915	103,393	77,853	68,399	42,435	27,466	1.6	1.0	0.8	1.0	0.8	0.7
Netherlands (Holland)	120,063	94,931	81,828	58,090	46,802	28,281	0.9	0.9	0.9	0.9	0.8	0.7
Norway	403,877	336,388	322,665	181,729	114,246	43,995	3.0	3.3	3.5	2.7	2.1	1.1
Portugal	59,360	30,608	15,996	8,138	4,542	4,116	0.4	0.3	0.2	0.1	0.1	0.1
Russia [1] and Finland	1,732,462	640,743	182,644	35,722	4,644	3,160	12.8	6.2	2.0	0.5	0.1	0.1
Scotland	261,076	233,524	242,231	170,136	140,835	108,518	1.9	2.3	2.6	2.5	2.5	2.6
Spain	22,108	7,050	6,185	5,121	3,764	4,244	0.2	0.1	0.1	0.1	0.1	0.1
Sweden	665,207	582,014	478,041	194,337	97,332	18,625	4.9	5.6	5.2	2.9	1.7	0.4
Switzerland	124,848	115,593	104,069	88,621	75,153	53,327	0.9	1.1	1.1	1.3	1.3	1.3
Turkey in Asia [1]	59,729	{9,910	{1,839	{1,205	{302	{128	0.4	{0.9	{(4)	{(4)	{(4)	{(4)
Turkey in Europe	32,230	}	}	}	}	}	0.2	}	}	}	}	}
Wales	82,488	93,586	100,079	83,302	74,533	45,763	0.6	0.9	1.1	1.2	1.3	1.1
All other countries [1]	158,992	95,062	200,153	93,985	41,943	70,704	1.2	0.9	2.2	1.4	0.8	1.7

[1] For the censuses from 1860 to 1880, inclusive, persons reported as born in Poland are included under "All other countries;" for the censuses of 1910 and 1900 (so far as possible), they are distributed under Austria, Germany, and Russia, respectively.
[2] Includes Newfoundland prior to 1910.
[3] Except Porto Rico.
[4] Less than one-tenth of 1 per cent.

TABLE 2: FOREIGN-BORN POPULATION, BY COUNTRY OF BIRTH: 1860 - 1910
(Thirteenth Census of the United States: Abstract, 190)

Table 1

CENSUS OF 1910 (APRIL 15).

YEAR OF IMMIGRATION.	Length of residence in United States, in years (y.) and months (m.).	Total foreign born. Number.	Per cent.	Foreign-born white. Number.	Per cent.
Total		13,515,886		13,345,545	
Year not reported		1,340,819		1,318,959	
Total with year reported.		12,175,067	100.0	12,026,586	100.0
1910, to Apr. 15	Less than 3½ m	233,852	1.9	231,696	1.9
1909	3½ m.–1 y. 3½ m.	579,419	4.8	573,585	4.8
1908	1 y. 3½ m.–2 y. 3½ m.	412,683	3.4	405,631	3.4
1907	2 y. 3½ m.–3 y. 3½ m.	706,771	5.8	694,362	5.8
1906	3 y. 3½ m.–4 y. 3½ m.	637,398	5.2	623,647	5.2
1905	4 y. 3½ m.–5 y. 3½ m.	530,808	4.4	520,161	4.3
1901–1904	5 y. 3½ m.–9 y. 3½ m.	1,505,214	12.4	1,479,844	12.3
1900 or earlier	9 y. 3½ m. or more	7,568,922	62.2	7,497,660	62.3
1906–1910	Less than 4 y. 3½ m	2,570,123	21.1	2,528,921	21.0
1901–1905	4 y. 3½ m.–9 y. 3½ m.	2,036,022	16.7	2,000,005	16.6
1896–1900	9 y. 3½ m.–14 y. 3½ m.	1,063,699	8.7	1,046,500	8.7
1891–1895	14 y. 3½ m.–19 y. 3½ m.	1,157,513	9.5	1,148,645	9.6
1890 or earlier	19 y. 3½ m. or more	5,347,710	43.9	5,302,515	44.1
1901–1910	Less than 9 y. 3½ m	4,606,145	37.8	4,528,926	37.7
1900 or earlier	9 y. 3½ m. or more	7,568,922	62.2	7,497,660	62.3
Distributing those with year not reported: Total		13,515,886	100.0	13,345,545	100.0
1901–1910	Less than 9 y. 3½ m	5,088,084	37.6	5,000,098	37.5
1900 or earlier	9 y. 3½ m. or more	8,427,802	62.4	8,345,447	62.5

CENSUS OF 1900 (JUNE 1).

YEAR OF IMMIGRATION.	Length of residence in United States, in years (y.) and months (m.).	Total foreign born. Number.	Per cent.	Foreign-born white. Number.	Per cent.
Total		10,341,276		10,213,817	
Year not reported		1,012,653		1,001,460	
Total with year reported.		9,328,623	100.0	9,212,357	100.0
1900, to June 1	Less than 5 m	201,128	2.2	192,607	2.1
1899	5 m.–1 y. 5 m.	235,410	2.5	229,315	2.5
1898	1 y. 5 m.–2 y. 5 m.	195,291	2.1	191,399	2.1
1897	2 y. 5 m.–3 y. 5 m.	172,288	1.8	169,117	1.8
1896	3 y. 5 m.–4 y. 5 m.	199,749	2.1	197,536	2.1
1895	4 y. 5 m.–5 y. 5 m.	214,577	2.3	212,198	2.3
1891–1894	5 y. 5 m.–9 y. 5 m.	1,144,654	12.3	1,136,842	12.3
1890 or earlier	9 y. 5 m. or more	6,965,526	74.7	6,883,343	74.7
1896–1900	Less than 4 y. 5 m.	1,003,866	10.8	979,974	10.6
1891–1895	4 y. 5 m.–9 y. 5 m.	1,359,231	14.6	1,349,040	14.6
1886–1890	9 y. 5 m.–14 y. 5 m.	1,596,030	17.1	1,585,062	17.2
1881–1885	14 y. 5 m.–19 y. 5 m.	1,566,448	16.8	1,546,825	16.8
1880 or earlier	19 y. 5 m. or more	3,802,148	40.8	3,751,456	40.7
1891–1900	Less than 9 y. 5 m.	2,363,097	25.3	2,329,014	25.3
1890 or earlier	9 y. 5 m. or more	6,965,526	74.7	6,883,343	74.7
Distributing those with year not reported: Total		10,341,276	100.0	10,213,817	100.0
1891–1900	Less than 9 y. 5 m.	2,609,173	25.2	2,571,196	25.2
1890 or earlier	9 y. 5 m. or more	7,732,103	74.8	7,642,621	74.8

TABLE 3: LENGTH OF RESIDENCE IN THE UNITED STATES

(Thirteenth Census of the United States: Abstract, 215)

FOREIGN-BORN WHITE POPULATION, BY YEAR OF ARRIVAL IN THE UNITED STATES, BY DIVISIONS AND STATES: 1910.

Table 2

DIVISION AND STATE.	YEAR OF IMMIGRATION.					PER CENT.[1]		
	1906–Apr.15, 1910	1901–1905	1891–1900	1890 or earlier.	Year unknown.	1906–1910	1901–1905	1900 or earlier.
United States.	2,538,921	2,000,005	2,195,145	5,302,515	1,318,959	21.0	16.6	62.3
GEOGRAPHIC DIVS.:								
New England...	369,442	283,246	390,564	686,607	84,527	21.4	16.4	62.3
Middle Atlantic...	1,095,778	906,454	904,348	1,577,972	341,627	24.4	20.2	55.4
E. North Central...	522,008	391,942	418,690	1,433,180	301,400	18.2	14.9	67.0
W. North Central...	186,544	155,683	195,365	836,626	239,013	13.6	11.3	75.1
South Atlantic...	56,884	40,259	40,322	98,320	54,770	24.1	17.1	58.8
E. South Central...	8,587	7,641	8,934	42,792	18,903	12.6	11.2	76.1
W. South Central...	49,857	34,596	48,929	121,484	93,893	19.6	13.6	66.9
Mountain...	90,961	58,916	63,082	159,212	64,739	24.4	15.8	59.7
Pacific...	148,860	121,268	124,911	346,322	120,087	20.1	16.4	63.6
NEW ENGLAND:								
Maine...	19,226	14,024	21,268	39,234	16,381	20.5	15.0	64.5
New Hampshire...	20,756	12,353	20,743	36,674	6,032	22.9	13.6	63.4
Vermont...	10,437	6,638	8,763	20,410	3,613	22.8	14.4	63.1
Massachusetts...	212,285	164,322	234,894	409,113	30,436	20.8	16.1	63.1
Rhode Island...	34,712	28,072	37,505	65,546	12,190	20.9	16.9	62.1
Connecticut...	72,026	57,837	67,391	115,630	15,875	23.0	18.5	58.5
MIDDLE ATLANTIC:								
New York...	598,583	516,519	542,974	907,939	163,257	23.3	20.1	56.5
New Jersey...	143,335	112,777	121,956	226,029	54,091	23.7	18.7	57.6
Pennsylvania...	353,860	277,158	239,418	444,004	124,279	26.9	21.1	52.0
E. N. CENTRAL:								
Ohio...	129,675	88,621	73,623	248,315	57,011	24.0	16.4	59.6
Indiana...	30,137	17,137	16,212	71,918	23,918	22.3	12.7	65.1
Illinois...	221,195	177,158	184,207	511,537	108,463	20.2	16.2	63.6
Michigan...	87,616	65,520	83,784	305,283	53,321	16.2	12.1	71.8
Wisconsin...	53,385	43,506	60,864	296,127	58,687	11.8	9.6	78.7
W. N. CENTRAL:								
Minnesota...	62,152	59,646	75,259	288,434	57,519	12.8	12.3	74.9
Iowa...	24,986	17,293	27,134	156,614	47,457	11.1	7.7	81.3
Missouri...	31,764	23,618	22,619	113,213	37,682	16.6	12.4	71.0
North Dakota...	20,397	23,744	27,906	58,922	25,189	15.6	18.1	66.3
South Dakota...	10,313	9,521	13,004	51,727	16,063	12.2	11.3	76.5
W. N. CEN.—Con.								
Nebraska...	19,726	12,738	18,113	99,686	25,602	13.1	8.5	78.4
Kansas...	17,206	9,123	11,330	68,030	29,501	16.3	8.6	75.1
SOUTH ATLANTIC:								
Delaware...	3,197	2,482	2,608	5,986	3,147	22.4	17.4	60.2
Maryland...	14,061	13,296	16,298	45,516	15,003	15.5	14.9	69.3
Dist. of Columbia	2,837	2,494	3,203	10,255	5,562	15.1	13.3	71.6
Virginia...	4,494	3,327	3,793	8,593	6,421	22.2	16.5	61.3
West Virginia...	22,623	10,869	5,818	9,794	7,968	46.1	22.1	31.8
North Carolina...	918	576	713	1,778	1,957	23.0	14.5	62.5
South Carolina...	642	536	654	2,205	2,017	15.9	13.3	70.8
Georgia...	1,822	1,746	2,112	5,067	4,325	17.0	16.2	66.8
Florida...	6,290	4,933	5,123	9,126	8,376	24.7	19.4	55.9
E. S. CENTRAL:								
Kentucky...	2,977	2,194	3,285	24,556	7,041	9.0	6.6	84.3
Tennessee...	1,878	1,800	2,069	8,152	4,560	13.5	13.0	73.5
Alabama...	2,673	2,479	2,379	6,821	4,664	18.6	17.3	64.1
Mississippi...	1,059	1,168	1,201	3,263	2,698	15.8	17.5	66.7
W. S. CENTRAL:								
Arkansas...	1,277	1,704	1,789	7,509	4,630	10.4	13.9	75.7
Louisiana...	4,188	5,571	8,720	18,260	15,043	11.4	15.2	73.4
Oklahoma...	4,410	3,082	4,452	16,609	11,531	15.4	10.8	73.8
Texas...	39,982	24,239	33,968	79,106	62,689	22.6	13.7	63.8
MOUNTAIN:								
Montana...	20,290	12,936	15,358	30,303	12,757	25.7	16.4	57.9
Idaho...	6,731	4,448	4,821	16,652	7,775	20.6	13.6	65.8
Wyoming...	7,829	4,783	3,826	7,945	2,735	32.1	19.6	48.3
Colorado...	22,095	16,678	19,944	51,408	16,726	20.1	15.1	64.8
New Mexico...	6,027	3,002	3,165	6,162	4,298	32.8	16.4	50.8
Arizona...	13,676	7,556	6,895	10,516	8,181	35.4	19.6	45.1
Utah...	10,493	6,650	6,657	29,320	10,273	19.8	12.5	67.7
Nevada...	3,820	2,863	2,416	6,906	1,994	23.9	17.9	58.2
PACIFIC:								
Washington...	43,444	35,450	33,917	85,031	43,355	22.0	17.9	60.1
Oregon...	18,772	13,040	13,178	40,622	17,389	21.9	15.2	62.8
California...	86,644	72,778	77,816	220,609	59,343	18.9	15.9	65.2

[1] Percentages based only on the number for whom the year of immigration was reported.

TABLE 4: FOREIGN-BORN WHITE POPULATION BY YEAR OF ARRIVAL, BY STATES, 1910

(Thirteenth Census of the United States: Abstract, 216)

Table 40	FOREIGN-BORN WHITE MALES 21 YEARS OF AGE AND OVER: 1910							
DIVISION AND STATE.	Naturalized.		Having first papers.		Alien.		Citizenship not reported.	
	Number.	Per cent.	Number.	Per cent.	Number.	Per cent.	Number.	Per cent.
United States	3,034,117	45.6	570,772	8.6	2,266,535	34.1	775,393	11.7
GEOGRAPHIC DIVS.:								
New England	323,994	40.7	48,508	6.1	366,161	45.9	58,184	7.3
Middle Atlantic	879,348	38.7	202,012	8.9	965,101	42.5	225,810	9.9
East North Central	812,490	51.6	148,254	9.4	426,278	27.1	186,322	11.8
West North Central	510,918	58.8	76,934	8.8	144,177	16.6	137,379	15.8
South Atlantic	61,134	40.6	8,997	6.0	57,127	37.9	23,407	15.5
East South Central	25,955	56.0	2,220	4.8	8,647	18.7	9,486	20.5
West South Central	70,765	41.2	10,071	5.9	52,853	30.7	38,251	22.2
Mountain	113,670	44.1	23,219	9.0	85,619	33.2	35,029	13.6
Pacific	235,844	46.4	50,557	9.9	160,572	31.6	61,525	12.1
NEW ENGLAND:								
Maine	14,994	30.9	1,490	3.1	23,672	48.8	8,308	17.1
New Hampshire	16,415	39.1	1,421	3.4	19,377	46.2	4,743	11.3
Vermont	10,811	45.5	1,164	4.9	9,652	40.6	2,132	9.0
Massachusetts	189,126	41.7	30,016	6.6	212,053	46.7	22,426	4.9
Rhode Island	32,040	42.2	5,314	7.0	31,996	42.2	6,549	8.6
Connecticut	60,608	39.6	9,103	5.9	69,431	45.3	14,026	9.2
MIDDLE ATLANTIC:								
New York	502,083	41.1	131,065	10.7	475,259	38.9	112,586	9.2
New Jersey	128,438	41.5	24,511	7.9	122,076	39.4	34,623	11.2
Pennsylvania	248,827	33.6	46,416	6.3	367,766	49.6	78,601	10.6
E. NORTH CENTRAL:								
Ohio	142,465	46.2	17,509	5.7	113,856	36.9	34,648	11.2
Indiana	42,533	47.8	13,320	15.0	18,354	20.6	14,720	16.6
Illinois	317,339	52.5	43,482	7.2	174,581	28.9	69,122	11.4
Michigan	167,304	55.4	26,235	8.7	76,550	25.3	32,088	10.6
Wisconsin	142,848	53.1	47,708	17.7	42,937	15.9	35,744	13.3
W. NORTH CENTRAL:								
Minnesota	179,187	60.1	26,222	8.8	58,132	19.5	34,741	11.6
Iowa	90,573	61.7	6,654	4.5	20,275	13.8	29,376	20.0
Missouri	65,612	54.0	10,117	8.3	25,835	21.3	19,840	16.3
North Dakota	46,636	58.5	9,824	12.3	10,965	13.8	12,296	15.4
South Dakota	32,495	59.6	8,020	14.7	4,376	8.0	9,637	17.7
Nebraska	57,270	60.7	9,924	10.5	12,347	13.1	14,804	15.7
Kansas	39,145	52.7	6,173	8.3	12,247	16.5	16,683	22.5
SOUTH ATLANTIC:								
Delaware	3,707	42.2	658	7.5	3,189	36.3	1,222	13.9
Maryland	24,256	50.6	3,278	6.8	13,573	28.3	6,866	14.3
Dist. of Columbia	6,474	55.2	1,058	9.0	2,304	19.6	1,902	16.2
Virginia	6,411	43.1	859	5.8	4,693	31.5	2,919	19.6
West Virginia	7,263	20.9	1,356	3.9	22,545	65.0	3,521	10.2
North Carolina	1,439	43.7	194	5.9	827	25.1	836	25.4
South Carolina	1,602	47.7	184	5.5	739	22.0	830	24.7
Georgia	4,023	47.3	625	7.3	1,846	21.7	2,019	23.7
Florida	5,959	34.2	783	4.5	7,411	42.5	3,292	18.9
E. SOUTH CENTRAL:								
Kentucky	13,225	64.7	815	4.0	2,754	13.5	3,646	17.8
Tennessee	5,444	53.8	464	4.6	1,867	18.5	2,337	23.1
Alabama	4,841	46.0	684	6.5	2,793	26.5	2,203	20.9
Mississippi	2,445	46.7	257	4.9	1,233	23.6	1,300	24.8
W. SOUTH CENTRAL:								
Arkansas	5,284	54.4	595	6.1	1,388	14.3	2,451	25.2
Louisiana	10,024	37.8	1,166	4.4	9,151	34.5	6,178	23.3
Oklahoma	12,074	51.3	1,477	6.3	4,449	18.9	5,551	23.6
Texas	43,383	38.7	6,833	6.1	37,865	33.8	24,071	21.5
MOUNTAIN:								
Montana	27,635	46.6	6,749	11.4	16,937	28.6	7,992	13.5
Idaho	12,817	49.6	2,478	9.6	6,215	24.0	4,334	16.8
Wyoming	6,837	37.4	1,937	10.6	8,125	44.5	1,364	7.5
Colorado	35,245	50.0	6,536	9.3	19,615	27.8	9,118	12.9
New Mexico	4,267	34.1	709	5.7	6,048	48.4	1,478	11.8
Arizona	5,912	23.0	1,113	4.3	14,574	56.7	4,083	15.9
Utah	15,351	47.0	2,415	7.4	9,626	29.5	5,260	16.1
Nevada	5,606	43.9	1,282	10.0	4,479	35.1	1,400	11.0
PACIFIC:								
Washington	68,895	46.8	15,258	10.4	43,202	29.3	19,869	13.5
Oregon	29,675	46.4	7,591	11.9	17,430	27.3	9,213	14.4
California	137,274	46.2	27,708	9.3	99,940	33.6	32,443	10.9

TABLE 5: FOREIGN-BORN WHITE MALES 21 YEARS AND OVER, NATURALIZED, HAVING FIRST PAPERS, OR ALIEN
(Thirteenth Census of the Untied States: Abstract, 117)

TABLE 2.—FOREIGN-BORN WHITE POPULATION OF THE UNITED STATES BY CITIZENSHIP AND COUNTRY OF BIRTH: 1930

COUNTRY OF BIRTH	Total foreign-born white	Naturalized	Having first papers	Alien	Unknown	Per cent naturalized
All countries....	13,366,407	7,859,193	1,246,521	3,787,086	473,607	58.8
England.............	808,672	541,880	66,858	165,179	34,755	67.0
Scotland.............	354,323	189,538	44,221	107,555	13,009	53.5
Wales.................	60,205	44,403	4,054	8,965	2,783	73.8
Northern Ireland.....	178,832	121,748	14,114	34,424	8,546	68.1
Irish Free State.......	744,810	492,191	65,413	144,178	43,028	66.1
Norway.............	347,852	246,735	29,954	59,054	12,109	70.9
Sweden.............	595,250	432,411	50,886	93,682	18,271	72.6
Denmark.............	179,474	134,513	15,519	23,506	5,936	74.9
Netherlands.........	133,133	88,725	11,996	28,234	4,178	66.6
Belgium.............	64,194	41,881	6,986	13,294	2,033	65.2
Switzerland..........	113,010	76,142	10,462	21,536	4,870	67.4
France..............	135,232	85,283	9,869	34,004	6,076	63.1
Germany.............	1,608,814	1,133,739	158,689	252,576	63,810	70.5
Poland..............	1,268,583	640,490	142,571	458,338	27,184	50.5
Czechoslovakia.......	491,638	301,401	44,504	133,379	12,354	61.3
Austria..............	370,914	233,582	31,876	91,298	14,158	63.0
Hungary.............	274,450	152,759	30,306	83,589	7,796	55.7
Yugoslavia...........	211,416	97,880	29,444	79,932	4,160	46.3
Russia..............	1,153,624	717,966	91,956	309,335	34,367	62.2
Lithuania............	193,606	91,875	22,736	74,547	4,448	47.5
Finland.............	142,478	72,709	15,754	50,489	3,526	51.0
Rumania............	146,393	88,277	15,553	39,173	3,390	60.3
Greece.............	174,526	78,059	25,112	65,977	5,378	44.7
Italy...............	1,790,424	894,647	143,380	705,892	46,505	50.0
Spain...............	58,302	11,045	6,824	38,539	1,894	18.9
Portugal............	69,974	13,062	4,875	49,994	2,043	18.7
Syria...............	57,227	29,133	5,889	20,454	1,751	50.9
Canada—French.....	370,852	173,938	29,797	154,002	13,115	46.9
Canada—Other.......	907,569	484,619	79,265	290,622	53,063	53.4
All other............	360,630	148,562	37,658	155,339	19,071	41.2

*TABLE 6: FOREIGN-BORN WHITE POPULATION BY
CITIZENSHIP AND COUNTRY OF BIRTH, 1930
(Fifteenth Census of the United States: Population, II, 403.)*

TABLE 37. DECLARATIONS OF INTENTION FILED, PETITIONS FOR NATURALIZATION FILED, AND ALIENS NATURALIZED: YEARS ENDED JUNE 30, 1907 TO 1947

	Declarations filed	Petitions filed			Aliens naturalized		
		Civilian	Military	Total	Civilian	Military	Total
1907-1947	7,993,428	6,328,504	471,025	6,799,529	5,851,694	464,603	6,316,297
1907-1910	526,322	164,036	-	164,036	111,738	-	111,738
1907 1/	73,658	21,113	-	21,113	7,941	-	7,941
1908	137,571	44,032	-	44,032	25,975	-	25,975
1909	145,745	43,141	-	43,141	38,374	-	38,374
1910	169,348	55,750	-	55,750	39,448	-	39,448
1911-1920	2,686,909	1,137,084	244,300	1,381,384	884,672	244,300	1,128,972
1911	189,249	74,740	-	74,740	56,683	-	56,683
1912	171,133	95,661	-	95,661	70,310	-	70,310
1913	182,095	95,380	-	95,380	83,561	-	83,561
1914	214,104	124,475	-	124,475	104,145	-	104,145
1915	247,958	106,399	-	106,399	91,848	-	91,848
1916	209,204	108,767	-	108,767	87,831	-	87,831
1917	440,651	130,865	-	130,865	88,104	-	88,104
1918	342,283	105,514	63,993	169,507	87,456	63,993	151,449
1919	391,156	128,523	128,335	256,858	89,023	128,335	217,358
1920	299,076	166,760	51,972	218,732	125,711	51,972	177,683
1921-1930	2,709,014	1,827,073	57,204	1,884,277	1,716,979	56,206	1,773,185
1921	303,904	177,898	17,636	195,534	163,656	17,636	181,292
1922	273,511	153,170	9,468	162,638	160,979	9,468	170,447
1923	296,636	158,059	7,109	165,168	137,975	7,109	145,084
1924	424,540	166,947	10,170	177,117	140,340	10,170	150,510
1925	277,218	162,258	-	162,258	152,457	-	152,457
1926	277,539	172,107	125	172,232	146,239	92	146,331
1927	258,295	235,298	5,041	240,339	195,493	4,311	199,804
1928	254,588	235,328	4,993	240,321	228,006	5,149	233,155
1929	280,645	254,799	720	255,519	224,197	531	224,728
1930	62,138	111,209	1,942	113,151	167,637	1,740	169,377
1931-1940	1,369,479	1,612,411	24,702	1,637,113	1,498,573	19,891	1,518,464
1931	106,272	142,249	3,225	145,474	140,271	3,224	143,495
1932	101,345	131,043	19	131,062	136,598	2	136,600
1933	83,046	110,604	2,025	112,629	112,368	995	113,363
1934	108,079	114,524	2,601	117,125	110,867	2,802	113,669
1935	136,524	131,378	-	131,378	118,945	-	118,945
1936	148,118	165,559	1,568	167,127	140,784	481	141,265
1937	176,195	157,670	7,794	165,464	162,923	2,053	164,976
1938	150,673	169,131	6,282	175,413	158,142	3,936	162,078
1939	155,691	213,413	-	213,413	185,175	3,638	188,813
1940	203,536	276,840	1,188	278,028	232,500	2,760	235,260
1941-1947	701,704	1,587,900	144,819	1,732,719	1,639,732	144,206	1,783,938
1941	224,123	277,807	-	277,807	275,747	1,547	277,294
1942	221,796	341,979	1,508	343,487	268,762	1,602	270,364
1943	115,664	338,885	38,240	377,125	281,459	37,474 2/	318,933
1944	42,368	275,486	50,231	325,717	392,766	49,213 2/	441,979
1945	31,195	172,905	23,012	195,917	208,707	22,695 2/	231,402
1946	28,787	110,071	13,793	123,864	134,849	15,213 2/	150,062
1947	37,771	70,767	18,035	88,802	77,442	16,462 2/	93,904

1/ From September 27, 1906 to June 30, 1907.
2/ Members of the armed forces include 1,425 naturalized overseas in 1943; 6,496 in 1944; 5,666 in 1945; 2,054 in 1946; and 5,370 in 1947.

United States Department of Justice
Immigration and Naturalization Service

TABLE 7: NATURALIZATION STATISTICS, 1907-1947
(Annual Report of the Immigration and Naturalization Service, Fiscal Year 1947)

STATE CENSUS RECORDS

Thirty-eight states had some form of census or enumeration. A census usually provides demographic data about individuals while an enumeration provides a listing of names, their residences, and sometimes an age, or age bracket. Consult *State Censuses, an Annotated Bibliography*, by Henry S. Dubester, or a second source, *State Census Records*, by Ann S. Lainhart[126] for a listing of states, or the appropriate state archives, to determine exact data fields used which reflect place of birth (both of the individual and of parents), or citizenship status. The 1905 and 1915 Iowa census asked for number of years in the United States and in Iowa, and the 1925 added, if naturalized. The 1925 Kansas census asked for the year of immigration and the year of naturalization. Massachusetts, in their 1865 census, asked if the individual was a "legal voter," or a "naturalized voter." Michigan, Minnesota, New York, Oregon, Rhode Island, Washington, and Wisconsin, as well as others, have censuses with data fields helpful to the genealogist in determining foreign birthplace or citizenship.

Appendix

III Internet Connections for Naturalization Research

The Internet is changing and growing so rapidly that web site addresses tend to become obsolete as fast as mercury runs through one's fingers. It is important, therefore, to know that there are both *locator* web sites in addition to individual web site addresses. The former consists of institutions or operators of search engines that can lead one to an appropriate federal, state, or county site. The National Archives and Records Administration maintains a permanent web site that provides on-line access to its newly published three volume *The Guide to Federal Records in the National Archives of the United States;* links to its Regional Records Service Facilities; and, where available, to each's regional archives *Guide.* Finally, it provides links to national genealogical web-sites. Each state maintains a web site which can connect the researcher to the state archives, library, or historical society. These can vary in degrees of assistance in locating naturalization records. Currently the Indiana State Archives maintains a direct link to all but Nebraska's state archival agencies. The USGenWeb project maintains links to state and county genealogical sources. The Allen County Public Library, Fort Wayne, Indiana, maintains a web list to genealogical resources found in each state; and Cyndi Howells maintains "Cyndi's List of Genealogy Sites on the Internet." There are many others. One will develop a personal access strategy using a favorite site or engine comfortable and easy to use. Many of these links overlap so there are several ways to access a single site.

Given the information available on the Internet, the ease of updating, and the speed of communication at low costs, use of the Internet to locate naturalization records has become the most efficient means of obtaining information about citizenship records.

NOTE: These Internet addresses often change.

National Archives and Records Administration (NARA) [www.nara.gov] also maintains ten Regional Records Services Facilities. The following sites hold naturalization records:

NARA'S Northeast Region (Boston) [www.nara.gov/regional/boston.html] has on-line its *Guide to Records in the National Archives-New England Region,* 1994.

NARA's Northeast Region (New York City) [www.nara.gov/regional/newyork.html] has on-line its *Guide to Records in the National Archives-Northeast Region,* 1994.

NARA's MidAtlantic Region (Center City Philadelphia) [www.nara.gov/regional/philacc.html] has on-line its *Guide to Records in the National Archives-Mid Atlantic Region*, 1994.

NARA's Southeast Region (Atlanta) [www.nara.gov/regional/atlanta.html] has on-line *Archival Holdings Related to Family History at NARA's Southeast Region*.

NARA's Great Lakes Region (Chicago) [www.nara.gov/regional/chicago.html] has on-line a separate listing of its naturalization holdings.

NARA's Central Plains Region (Kansas City) [www.nara.gov/regional/kansas.html] has on-line its *Guide to Records in the National Archives Central Plains Region*, 1994.

NARA's Southwest Region (Fort Worth) [www.nara.gov/regional/ftworth.html] has on-line its *Guide to Records in the National Archives-Southwest Region*, 1994.

NARA's Rocky Mountain Region (Denver) [www.nara.gov/regional/denver.html] has on-line its *Guide to Records in the National Archives-Rocky Mountain Region*, 1996.

NARA'S Pacific Region (San Francisco) [www.nara.gov/regional/sanfranc.html] has on- line its *Guide to Records in the National Archives-Sierra Region*, 1995.

NARA's Pacific Alaska Region (Seattle) [www.nara.gov/regional/seattle.html] has on-line its *Guide to Records in the National Archives-Pacific Northwest Region*, 1994.

NARA's Pacific Region (Laguna Niguel) [www.nara.gov/regional/laguna.html] has on-line its *Guide to Records in the National Archives-Pacific Southwest Region*, 1996.

State Agencies: [www.ai.irg/icpr/webfile/archives/arclinks.html]. This web site is available through the Indiana State Archives home page, [www.ai.org/icpr/webfile/archives/homepage.html].

U.S.Genweb: [www.usgenweb.com.html]

Cyndi's list of genealogical sites on the web: [www.CyndisList.com]

Allen County Public Library, Fort Wayne, Indiana: [www.acpl.lib.in.us/Genealogy/genealogy_sites.html]

The Immigration and Naturalization Service Website: [www.ins.usdoj.gov]

Appendix

IV Definition of Select Terms

[The Immigration and Naturalization Service has a glossary of terms available on the Internet (www.ins.usdoj.gov/glossary/index.html). These provide the official and legal, rather than the following historical, definitions of immigration and citizenship words.]

Affidavit A written statement verifying residence and good moral character of a naturalization petitioner, made voluntarily, and confirmed by oath, by two citizens of the United States. Affidavits, sometimes attached to the Petition for Naturalization, or filed separately, have been made when witnesses could not appear at the court hearing.

Alien Any person not a citizen or national of the United States (66 Stat. 163, section 101).

Alien Registration "It shall be the duty of every alien now or hereafter in the United States, who (1) is fourteen years or older, (2) who has not been registered and fingerprinted under section 30, and (3) remains in the United States for thirty days or longer, to apply for registration and to be fingerprinted before the expiration of such thirty days" (54 Stat. 653-674, 8 U.S. C. 452, Act of June 28, 1940, effective August 27). Public Law 97-116, December 29,1981, 95 Stat.1617, repealed the requirement for annual registration of aliens every January.

Alien Registration Card A certificate of alien registration was required to be carried by all aliens over the age of eighteen. After January, 1941, reference to the number was made on naturalization records. The Alien Registration Number is the number used in filing and retrieving naturalization information about the individual after April 1, 1944.

Certificate of Arrival Under the Naturalization law June 29, 1906, each alien was registered at the point of entry. Such registry provided for "name, age, occupation, personal description (including height, complexion, color of hair and eyes), the place of birth, the last residence, the intended place of residence in the United

States, and the date of arrival of said alien, and if he or she entered through a port, the name of the vessel in which he or she comes" (34 Stat. 596). This act also provided that a certificate from the Naturalization Service showing data from the certificate of arrival be made a part of the petition for naturalization until July 1, 1929, then on the declaration thereafter.

Certificate of Naturalization "The title to citizenship is the recorded order of the court. The certificate is simply the conclusive evidence of such order" [*Report of the Department of Labor, 1914*, 564]. Issued formally after September 27, 1906, this document was given to the newly naturalized citizen as proof of citizenship. A duplicate was sent to Washington, and a stub was maintained in book form by the clerk of court, until after 1925, when the stub served as an index card.

Court of Record A federal, state, or local court, that under the 1790 statute "having common law jurisdiction, and a seal and clerk or prothonotary," and under the 1906 and later laws "having a seal, a clerk, and jurisdiction in actions at law or equity, or law and equity, in which the amount in controversy is unlimited." Courts no longer could naturalize after disposing of petitions filed before October 1, 1991. After that date, a naturalization court is one "authorized to *award* U.S. citizenship."

Declaration of Intention The first step in becoming a naturalized citizen. In use in the United States from 1795 until 1952 (and voluntary thereafter). Alien filed a statement under oath that it was "bona fide his or her intention to become a citizen of the United States, and to renounce all allegiance" to his or her former head of state. Contents of the declaration have varied greatly until September 27, 1906, when the federal government standardized the form. "The declaration of intention is a sworn statement by the alien that it is his intention in good faith to become a citizen of the United States, to reside permanently therein, and that he will, before being admitted to citizenship, renounce forever all foreign allegiance . . . to the sovereignty of which he is a citizen or subject." [Lecture 12, 3; 1906 Act, sec. 4, as amended, Act of 1929].

Derivative Citizenship Citizenship based upon the citizenship of another, as the wife of a husband or a minor under the age of twenty-one, upon the citizenship of the father.

Enemy Alien "Aliens who are natives, denizens, citizens, or subjects of countries with which the United States is at war." Acts of Congress affected these aliens, during the War of 1812, and the major conflicts in the twentieth century.

Federal Circuit Court Created as part of the Judiciary act of 1789 and abolished effective December 31, 1911. Although it had limited jurisdiction, it naturalized. Not to be confused with "circuit courts" found in some states.

Final Papers Informal name given to the "Petition for Naturalization."

First Papers Informal name given to the "Declaration of Intention."

Foreign-born Persons   "Foreign-born persons include those born outside of the United States and its outlying territories; namely, Alaska, Hawaii, Puerto Rico, Philippine Islands, Guam, American Samoa, Panama Canal Zone, and Virgin Islands of the United States." (See 1930 census instructions.)

Minor's Citizenship   "Minor" referred to a person under the age of twenty-one. From 1824 - 1906, minor aliens who had lived in the United States three years before the age of twenty one, and for two years thereafter, could make application for naturalization without a previously filed declaration of intention but were required to file it at the time of admission.

Naturalization   Conferring of nationality of a state upon a person after birth by any means whatsoever (8 U.S. C. 907). "Naturalization is the act of adopting a foreigner, and clothing him with the privileges of a native citizen" *Boyd v. Thayer* (1892) 143 U.S. 135, 162.

Petition   Formal renunciation of allegiance to a foreign head of state and the taking of an oath to support the Constitution of the United States, done before a court of record, "which proceedings shall be recorded by the clerk of the court" (Acts of April 14, 1802 and May 26, 1824). Sometimes referred to as "second papers" or "final papers." Generally after the early 1850's some courts recorded the petition in separate ledgers and after 1906, the form was prescribed by the federal government.

Registry   From 1798 to 1828 a separate document providing demographic data about himself and family (wife and minor children) [See pages 23-24]. Also under the Naturalization Act of 1906, a registry requirement for aliens, generating a "Certificate of Arrival" (see above). A Certificate of Registry issued after July 1, 1929 to those with no evidence of arrival before June 2, 1921 (later before July 1, 1924).

Second Papers   Informal name given to the Petition for Naturalization.

Naturalization Inventory Checklist

The problem in seeking naturalization records is determining **if** an ancestor sought first or second papers. Combine knowledge on the personal life of the individual with information on the citizenship process to reduce uncertainty. Second, define a time period. Third, use biographical, migrational, and neighborhood information to refine possible locations where, if applicable, registry, declaration, or petition proceedings may have been filed.

Use this worksheet as a *model* and modify it to meet specific needs as known information dictates. It is designed to link personal times, places, and events in an ancestor's life to specific naturalization laws and proceedings in force at the corresponding time and place.

NAME [LAST]: (Actual spelling) _____

(Soundex spelling) _____

(Variant spellings) _____

(Truncated spelling) _____

(Name changes) _____
More likely if person "subject of" rather than "citizen of" and after 1906 naturalization law.

NAME [FIRST]: (In native language) _____

(English variations) _____

(Nick names) _____

(Transposing middle for first) _____

BIRTH DATE [ACTUAL OR APPROXIMATE]: _____

POSSIBLE CENSUS YEARS: 1790   1800   1810   1820   1830   1840   1850

                                         1860   1870   1880   1890   1900   1910   1920

[Check Appendix II for questions asked of foreign-born.]
[1890 includes veteran's census]
[state census records]:   State: _____

                                  State: _____

DEATH DATE [ACTUAL OR APPROXIMATE]: _____

EVIDENCE OR CENSUS DATA INDICATING FILING FIRST OR SECOND PAPERS: _____
_____

NATURALIZATION LAWS IN EFFECT DURING LIFE TIME [SEE APPENDIX I]: _____
_____
_____

WHAT MOTIVATED POSSIBLE FILING OF DECLARATION OR PETITION:

Landownership/Homestead: _____
[Check State Laws to see if filing a declaration required]

Voting Privileges: _____
[Check State Laws to see if filing a declaration required]

Military Service: _____

"Enemy Alien" Statutes: _____
[War 1812; WWI; WWII]

Nationality: _____
[Census records show % of each nationality likely to seek citizenship—Appendix II]

Desire to return to native county to visit: _____

LOCATION:

How long a resident in locality where died: _____

Where did neighbors come from: _____
[Check county histories and census records for migration patterns]

What was likely port of arrival: _____

    [Check naturalization papers in county for same nationality to see at what port they arrived]

Possible Previous Residences: _____

    [State, Region, County, City]

Likelihood of Employment: _____

    [Canal/Railroad building; marble or other skilled occupations]

NATURALIZATION RECORDS:

Relate individual's times, locations, and personal events to naturalization laws in effect *during ancestor's entire lifetime* and relate to broad naturalization record keeping patterns--1790's - 1850's; 1850's - 9-26-1906; 9-27-1906 - forward:

Registry Required (1798 - 1828)	yes	no
Declaration waived by law or minor's status [check for each law]	yes	no
Citizen by marriage (1855 - 1907)	yes	no
Military service exemption [Civil War, other wars]	yes	no
Certificate of Arrival (6/29/1906 - +)	yes	no
Certificate of Registry (7/01/1929 - +)	yes	no

Local Naturalization Traditions

    Which courts did most of the naturalization proceedings at what times? _____

    County Level

    [Create list of all courts in existence during ancestor's life time in jurisdiction--federal, state, local]

Naturalization Records

Check permanent records of court [Minute & Order Books, esp. pre-1850's]	yes	no
When were separate ledgers used?	date:	_____
As federally mandated records 9/27/1906	yes	no
Personal possession of a declaration,	yes	no
certificate of arrival	yes	no
preliminary application	yes	no
Check the "loose papers" of the court	yes	no

Are records centralized?	yes	no
which ones? _____		
where? _____		
Are records indexed [WPA, other]?	yes	no
Are records abstracted & published?	yes	no
Are records listed [Internet, by name, state or county]?	yes	no
Lost by destruction of courthouse?	yes	no
Could declaration be filed elsewhere?	yes	no
Are records copied?	yes	no
LDS Family History Library	yes	no
Immigration and Naturalization Service	yes	no
Elsewhere	yes	no

Ask these questions unique to your ancestor to link him or her to naturalization laws, courts, records, and proceedings.

NATURALIZATION INVENTORY

I. [1790] - 9-26-1906

    A. Declaration of Intention [1795 - 1906]

        1. Declaration of Intention "First Papers" ledgers (1820's - 1906, as found)

        2. Declaration of Intention Naturalization papers

    B. Petition for Naturalization

        1. Petition, "Second Papers" "Final Record" ledgers (ca. 1850's - 1906, as found)

        2. Petition papers

        3. Petition for Naturalization Order Books, under Acts of Congress, March 3, 1903 (ledger, 1903-1906)

        4. Application for Naturalization "Statements and Affidavits" under 1903 Act 1903-1906, (papers), as found.

        5. Separate "Alien Children Exempt from Filing Declaration of Intention Petition" ledger ca. 1860- 1906.

C. Any General Indexes

    1. ledgers

    2. card files

    3. lists

II. 9-27-1906 - current

  A. Declaration of Intention

    1. Ledger, Form 2202 series, l906 - 6-30-1929

    2. Ledger, Form 2202 L-A, 7/01/1929 - 1/12/1941

    3. Ledger, Form N-315, 1/13/1941 - + (Note: generally eliminated after 1952)

    4. Misc. Declaration and supporting papers

  B. Petition for Naturalization

    1. Ledger, Form 2204 series, 1906 -6/30/1929

    2. Ledger, Form 2204 L-A, 7/01/1929 - 1/12/1941

    3. Ledger, Form N-405, 1/13/1941 - +

    4. Misc. Naturalization papers, as Certificates of Arrival, Witness Affidavits, etc.

  C. Certificates

    1. Stubs, 1906 - ca. 1925 (perhaps to 6/30/1929) (ledgers)

    2. Individual 3" X 5" "Index Cards" ca. 1925 - +

  D. Forms 2228, 2229, and Court Orders

  E. Papers, files, jackets

  F. Correspondence related to individuals

CROSS REFERENCES

A. Court Order Books

B. Entry Dockets/Fee Books

C. Case Files

 **Notes**

1. *The American Heritage Dictionary* (Boston: Houghton Mifflin, 1981), 548.

2. William Dollarhide, "Genealogy Source Checklist," *Genealogy Bulletin* 20 (October/November/December 1993): 10-12. Gives a checklist of over 400 "life events" a genealogist should consult.

3. Dorothea N. Spear, *Bibliography of American Directories Through 1860* (Worcester, MA: American Antiquarian Society, 1961) and *City Directories of the United States, 1860 - 1901: Guide to the Microfilm* (Woodbridge, CT: Research Publications, 1983). Microfiche of city directories through 1860 are in many libraries and roll microfilm of directories for 79 major cities are available through 1935. City directories can offer pleasant surprises. The 1825 City Directory for Cincinnati shows place of birth, by state or country, for each person; early twentieth century directories for Springfield, Illinois, have death dates. After WWI, many directories show the first name and initial of maiden surname of wives. Check not only the alphabetical listing, but "erratica" and the cross listing arranged by address.

4. Government Printing Office, 1909. Chapter 10 has an excellent discussion on the origin of surnames (111-115) and Table 111: "Nomenclature, Dealing with Names Represented by at Least 100 White Persons, by States and Territories, at the First Census: 1790," 227-270, provides a listing of names and variant spellings. The book as been reprinted by Heritage Quest, Bountiful, UT, 1989, and the list has been reprinted as *Surnames Listed in the 1790 United States Census,* (Bountiful, Utah: Heritage Quest, n. d.).

5. *Reports of the Department of Labor, 1914* (Washington: Government Printing Office, 1915), 564.

6. See bibliographical essay, part 2.

7. *Fifth Census or Enumeration of the Inhabitants of the United States, 1830* (Washington: Duff Green, 1832), 163. White foreigners not naturalized were 107,832 of a total of free white males and females of 10,526,248. See also William J. Bromwell, *History of Immigration to the United States* (New York: Arno Press reprint, 1969), 14-16 and Table, 175. From such calculations, about 190,000 alien *male passengers* arrived, 1790-1828, of which about 62 percent were not yet naturalized as of the 1830 census. About 2,500-4,000 names potentially were sent to the U.S. Secretary of State under the 1798 naturalization act and perhaps 25,000 to 30,000 reports and registries were filed, 1798-1828. These figures are approximations only, based on immigration and census statistics.

8. U.S. Department of Commerce, Bureau of the Census, *Fifteenth Census of the United States: 1930.* Population Volume 2: Population (Washington: Government Printing Office, 1933), Table 4, 405. The naturalization statistics for 1900 and 1910 are limited to free white males 21 and over, as opposed to the 1920 and 1930 censuses where white foreign-born residents of all ages are included. Of the 13,345,545 white foreign-born residents of all ages and gender, in 1910, 6, 646,817 were free white males. Of these 3,034,117, or 45.6 %, were naturalized and 2, 266,535 were aliens. But, to compare properly the 1910 data to the 1920 and 1930 statistics, the actual percentage of all naturalized male foreign-born, was 34.1. The chart for females, 1920 and 1930, shows an increase in the number of women who became naturalized under the 1922 law requiring them to seek citizenship on their own.

9. *Reports of the Department of Labor, 1914,* 540.

10. "All persons born in the United States and not subject to any foreign power, excluding Indians not taxed, are declared to be citizens of the United States."

11. C. R. Riddiough, "Documentary Evidence of Citizenship Status," *Lecture 25* (December 3, 1934): 1. Immigration and Naturalization Service, (Washington: Government Printing Office, 1934).

12. Act of April 14, 1802, 2 Stat. 153, sec. 3. See also Act of March 26, 1790, 1 Stat. 103, sec. 1 and Act of January 29, 1795, 1 Stat. 414, sec. 1 (First).

13. Act of June 29, 1906, 34 Stat. 596, sec. 3; Act of October 14, 1940, 54 Stat. 1137, sec. 301(a), Act of June 27, 1952, 66 Stat. 163, sec. 310(a). The 1906 act clarified the interpretation of a "court of record" by restricting naturalization to courts having unlimited civil jurisdiction only, thus reducing the number of courts exercising naturalization jurisdiction. See also page 10 and note 19.

14. U.S., Congress, Senate, Committee on Immigration, *A Report and Recommendations From the Secretary of State on the Subject of the Naturalization of Aliens in the United States,* 58th Congress, 3d Session, Vol. 2, Document No. 63, January 5, 1905, 18-27, illustrates a variety of naturalization forms used by a number of courts.

15. Some courts still entered the naturalization order in the court's official record in addition to proper entry in the Petition for Naturalization, Form 2204. See, for example, Hamilton County, Indiana, Circuit Court, Civil Order Books, Volume 51, 190, 291, and 447. The cancellation of naturalization in a letter from the Immigration and Naturalization Service in 1948 was attached to the 1907 Order Book entry and not the Petition Record, Form 2204, and also, Volume 61, 289. Many courts also referred to the order as an entry in the court's fee or docket ledger, usually for accounting purposes. If the appropriate naturalization record is missing, this may provide an alternative reference.

16. U.S. Circuit Courts were abolished effective after December 31, 1911. Act of March 3, 1911, 36 Stat. 1167, sec. 289. This act took affect January 1, 1912.

17 For the state of New York, the trial courts of general jurisdiction and most likely to have exercised naturalization jurisdiction are called *Supreme Courts.* The parallel to other states' Supreme Courts, in New York, is the Court of Appeals. Researchers must check the records of New York's Supreme Courts, found in the counties, as they would other states' district or circuit courts.

18. The naturalization records of the Indiana Supreme Court are in the Indiana State Archives, Indiana Commission on Public Records and those for Minnesota in the Minnesota Research Center and the Nebraska

Historical Society. Paula Stuart Warren, "Genealogical Research in Minnesota", *National Genealogical Society Quarterly*, 77 (March 1989), 38; Sylvia Nimmo, "Nebraska Research," *National Genealogical Society Quarterly*, 77 (December 1989), 272.

19. For a legal discussion of what constitutes a court of record, see U.S., Congress, House Committee on the Judiciary, *Naturalization Certificates Issued by the Municipal Court of Biddleford, Me.: Report to Accompany H.R. 2707*, 52d Congress, 2d session, December 20, 1892, Report No. 2180, Volume 1, 4. The discussion excludes certain courts as courts of records, including Probate Courts. See page 10 of text and note 21.

20. U.S. Congress, House, Committee on Immigration and Naturalization, *Report to the President of the Commission on Naturalization*, 59th Congress, 1st Session, Volume 44, document No.46, submitted November 8, 1905, 88.

21. *Annual Report of the Attorney General of the United States, 1903* (Washington: Government Printing Office, 1903), 397. For an example of a certificate issued by an Ohio Probate Court, see Arlene Eakle and Johni Cerny, editors, *The Source: A Guidebook of American Genealogy* (Salt Lake City: Ancestry Publishing Co., 1984), 38. The revised edition of 1997 does not contain this illustration.

22. *Reports of the Department of Commerce and Labor, 1907* (Washington: Government Printing Office, 1907), 195; *1908*, 287; *1909*, 298; *1910*, 365.

23. *Ibid., 1907*, 195.

24. Auditor's Office, Greene County Courthouse, Bloomfield, Indiana, Commissioners' Record C, 11.

25. *Reports of the Department of Labor, 1932*, 107. Of these, 2,064 courts (1803 state and 261 federal) actually were exercising naturalization jurisdiction.

26. *Directory of Courts Having Jurisdiction in Naturalization Proceedings, United States Department of Justice, Immigration and Naturalization Service, October 15, 1963*, Publication M-93, 1. The Genealogical Society has this publication on microfilm, roll 1730286.

27. *Basic Guide to Naturalization*, United States Department of Justice, Immigration and Naturalization Service, publication M 230, 4. The last field reflects automatic citizenship when territory was annexed.

28. If any lists were sent to the Secretary of State, these apparently were lost in the Washington, DC, fire during the War of 1812, or later. No lists appear in the *American State Papers* series or publications from the National Archives, listing manuscript or microfilm holdings from the Secretary of State's office.

29. *Report to the President of the Commission on Naturalization*, 66. Appendix C surveys state laws regarding naturalization.

30. *Ibid.*, 87-88, 92.

31. *Annual Report of the Attorney General, 1903*, 398.

32. Act of June 29, 1906, 34 Stat. 596, Preamble.

33. Department of Commerce and Labor, Division of Naturalization, Circular 126, *Rules and Regulations Relating to the Enforcement of the Naturalization Law*, August 25, 1906, 2. See also page 47 regarding use of unauthorized certificate of naturalization forms.

34. *U.S. Department of Justice, Annual Report of the Immigration and Naturalization Service, 1950, 81; 1951, 98; and 1954,.* 60. See also Bertam M. Bernard, "United States Immigration and Naturalization Service," *The Pennsylvania Genealogical Magazine,* XXVI-2 (1969), 120-21.

35. Act of June 27, 1952, 66 Stat. 163, 8 U.S.C.A. For general literature on procedures for naturalization see *Naturalization Requirements and General Information,* N-17 and for sample forms see *Basic Guide to Naturalization,* Form M-230, both published by the Immigration and Naturalization Service, and are available at local offices. The declarations of intention were still filed with clerks and were to have been kept in separate ledgers (sec. 339e). Courts which continued to naturalize after 1952 have relatively few declarations but for each person there will be a petition in a separate book.

36. Public Law 101-649, passed November 29, 1990, 104 Stat. 4968.

37. *Reports of the Department of Labor, 1918, 588.*

38. *Ibid.,* 613-14.

39. Act of June 8, 1926, 44 Stat. 709.

40. *Ibid.* Many local courts cited this law as reason for ceasing naturalization procedures. The change in forms and procedures effective July 1, 1929, served as a catalyst. This act permitted Federal District Court judges to appoint preliminary naturalization examiners. There also is an appearance of termination of naturalization since ledger book entries for Forms 2202 and 2204 were canceled. However, numbers continue from the old ledger to those created on new forms.

41. *Reports of the Department of Labor, 1913, 372.*

42. Statistical data from Indiana courts indicate that about 40 percent of local courts continued to naturalize after 1929. This percentage varies from state to state. Oregon had courts in at least three counties naturalize into the 1970's. See *Bulletin, Genealogical Forum of Portland, Oregon,* XXXIV-3 (March 1985), 117-18. The Oregon State Archives has accessioned many of these records; see individual counties for terminal dates of exercising their naturalization jurisdictions.

43. *Report of the Commissioner of Immigration and Naturalization,* for the year ending June 30, 1960, Immigration and Naturalization Service, Washington, 10-11.

44. The new Declaration of Intention Form, 2202 L-A, added spouse, marriage date, place, spouse's birth date, and names of children, with birth dates, places and residences. It also asked for data on previous declarations and last foreign residence. The Petition, 2204 L-A, changed less, asking, for example, for the petitioner's last foreign address. Most of the new questions on the declaration were formerly asked on the old petition, Form 2204. See Illus. 11 and 12 and Illus. 14 and 15.

45. For additional information see Leigh L. Nettleton, "Naturalization Procedure, Including Certificate of Arrival, Declaration of Intention, Petition for Naturalization, and Certificate of Citizenship," *Lecture 12* (April 23, 1934). U.S. Department of Labor, Immigration and Naturalization Service (Washington: Government Printing Office, 1924).

46. *West's Indiana Digest 2d,* (St. Paul, MN: West Publishing, 1991).

47. 6 Blackf 341. If Wynn had filed his registry required under the 1802 act, the 1804 law permitting derivative citizenship (page 53) would have applied and the descendants of Wynn and Eldon never would have had this lawsuit.

48. Act of April 14, 1802, 2 Stat. 153, sec. 2. This section was part of the naturalization process and not the immigration process. The first immigration act requiring statistical data was the Act of March 7, 1819. The first registry was required by the Act of June 18, 1798, 1 Stat. 566, sec. 4.

49. Act of March 22, 1816, 3 Stat. 259 sec. 1; Act of May 24, 1824, 4 Stat. 69, sec. 2 legalized certificates failing to comply with the Act of March 22, 1816.

50. National Archives and Records Service, Special List 31: *List of Pre-1840 Federal District and Circuit Court Records,* 1972, 4-5.

51. Roy C. Turnbaugh, Jr. *A Guide to County Records in the Illinois Regional Archives* (Springfield, IL: The Illinois State Archives, 1983), 156.

52. *Report to the President of the Commission on Naturalization,* 82-83. For a historical treatise on the New York City voter-naturalization frauds , see Pamelia S. Olson, "Naturalization and Voter Registration Frauds in New York City 1855-1870," *Heritage Quest* 62 (Mar/Apr 1996), 64-67. Fraud also was exposed in New York City in December, 1933.

53. *Annual Report of the Attorney General, 1903,* 394.

54. *Reports of the Department of Commerce and Labor, 1910* (Washington: Government Printing Office, 1911), 368.

55. *Report to the President of the Commission on Naturalization,* 89.

56. *Annual Report of the Attorney General, 1903,* 395.

57. C. H. Riddiough, "Documentary Evidence of Citizenship Status," *Lecture 25* (December 3, 1934): 2. Immigration and Naturalization Service, (Washington: Government Printing Office, 1935).

58. *Reports of the Department of Commerce and Labor, 1908* (Washington: Government Printing Office, 1909), 301.

59. *Report to the President of the Commission on Naturalization,* 18. These records evidently were incomplete as later laws adjusted naturalization procedures due to faulty certificates of arrival.

60. J. Henry Wagner, "Nature, Interrelations, and Use of Immigration and Naturalization Documents," *Lecture 13* (April 30, 1934): 6. Immigration and Naturalization Service, (Washington: Government Printing Office, *1934*).

61. *Reports of the Department of Labor, 1914,* 555.

62. Form 2204, the Petition, was changed in 1910 to include any marriage of petitioner or birth of children after the time of filing the declaration to the date of filing the petition.

63. *Reports of the Department of Labor, 1914,* 564.

64. *Report to the President of the Commission on Naturalization,* 36.

65. *Lecture 25,* 2.

66. See Lecture series: Edward J. Shaughnessy, "Legislative Background and Administration of the Registry of Aliens Act of March 2, 1929," *Lecture 4* (March 5, 1934); Leigh L. Nettleton, "Naturalization Procedure, Including Certificate of Arrival, Declaration of Intention, Petition for Naturalization, and Certificate of Citizenship," *Lecture 12* (April 23, 1934); J. Henry Wagner, "Nature, Interrelation, and Use of Immigration and Naturalization Documents, *Lecture 13* (April 30, 1934); and C. R. Riddiough, "Documentary Evidence of Citizenship Status," *Lecture 25* (December 3, 1934). (Washington: Government Printing Office.) Form numbers, comments, and procedures for I through VI are taken from these lectures.

67. Aliens began applying for certificates of arrival five years after the effective date of the 1906 Act, or after September 27, 1911. See *Reports of the Department of Commerce and Labor, 1911*, 387-88. The report called this process "onerous" due to "clerical errors in the records, such as misspelled names, erroneous dates, and measurements."

68. Edward J. Shaughnessey, "Legislative Background and Administration of the Registry of Aliens' Act of March 2, 1929," *Lecture 4* (March 5, 1934): 4. (Washington: Government Printing Office, 1934).

69. The directories for 1932 and 1963 give the individual number of courts. These served as a basis for the Bureau's filing system.

70. C. R. Riddiough, "Documentary Evidence of Citizenship Status," *Lecture 25* (December 3, 1934): 6. Immigration and Naturalization Service (Washington: Government Printing Office, 1935).

71. *Report, 1931*, 72.

72. *Reports of the Department of Labor, 1913*, 378.

73. *Ibid*, 16.

74. *Reports of the Department of Labor, 1913*, 356-59.

75. Department of Labor, Immigration and Naturalization Service, *Lecture 13* (12, April 30, 1934):12. See also J.J. Kunna and H.L. Stanforth "Immigration and Naturalization Statistics of the United States--Their Nature, Volume, and Method of Compilation," *Lecture 30* (January 1, 1934). Immigration and Naturalization Service, (Washington: Government Printing Office, 1934). From September 27, 1906 through June 30, 1934, 6,320,987 declarations versus 3,935,987 petitions were filed.

76. Putnam County, Indiana, *Declaration of Intentions*, Form 2202, (1906 - 1929), 27.

77. *Acts of the Indiana General Assembly*, 1911, Chapter 150, effective for the general election in 1912. Section 9 required registration forms, including one for foreign-born applications not naturalized but who had declared his intention. The form required his age and birth date, place of birth, when arrived in the United States, when and where he filed his declaration, and his residences given in specific detail. Duell was one of 4,351 who filed, probably to be able to vote [see note 74].

78. For additional information see "Derivative Citizenship—Law and Practice," *Lecture 34* (February 5, 1935). U.S. Department of Labor, Immigration and Naturalization Service.

79. Act of March 26, 1790, 1 Stat. 103, sec. 1; Act of January 29, 1795, 1 Stat. 414, sec. 3; Act of April 14,1 802,2 Stat. 153, sec. 4; Act of October 14, 1940, 54 Stat. 1137, sec. 504. However, secs. 313-315 reinstated and refined this provision. Act of June 27, 1952, 66 Stat. 163, secs. 320-322. See Appendix I for additional information.

80. Act of February 10, 1855, 10 Stat. 604, sec. 2.

81. *Reports of the Department of Labor, 1915,* 383.

82. *Reports of the Department of Labor, 1929,* 69.

83. *Reports of the Department of Labor, 1930, 86; 1932,* 105.

84. *Annual Report of the Commissioner of Naturalization,* fiscal year ending June 30, 1927 (Washington: Government Printing Office, 1927), 13.

85. Act of July 17, 1862, 12 Stat. 597, sec. 21.

86. Department of the Interior, Census Division, *Abstract of the Eleventh Census, 1890,* second edition (Washington: Government Printing Office, 1896), Table 31, 84.

87. Act of July 26, 1894, 28 Stat. 123, sec. 1, "Pay of the Navy."

88. Act of June 7, 1872, 17 Stat. 268, sec. 2. *Reports of the Department of Commerce and Labor, 1909,* 26.

89. Act of August 1, 1894, 28 Stat. 215, sec. 2.

90. Act of May 9, 1918, 40 Stat. 542, sec. 1

91. *Reports of the Department of Labor, 1918,* 200 and 613.

92. *Reports of the Department of Labor, 1919,* 770.

93. *Reports of the Department of Labor, 1918,* 200. Many of these were done by federal courts. The National Archives, Great Lakes Region, Chicago, has Military and Petition books and records for World War I for federal courts at Hammond, Indiana, and Chicago, Illinois, and for World War II for such courts at Chicago, Peoria, Springfield, and Danville, Illinois, and Detroit and Marquette, Michigan. The LDS Family History Library has two rolls of microfilm of "Military Petitions for Naturalization, 1918-1921," from the Geary County Kansas District Court. This is the location of Fort Riley.

94. Immigration and Naturalization Service, [www.ins.usdoj.gov/natz/special.html].

95. *Second Report of the Provost Marshal General to the Secretary of War on the Operation of the Selective Service System to December 20, 1918,* (Washington: Government Printing Office, 1919), 88.

96. *Ibid.,* 89, Tables 20, 21 and 22.

97. *Ibid.,* Appendix, T. Table 23-D, 399, and text pages 104-107.

98. *Acts of the Indiana General Assembly:* 1817/1818, Chap. 25, sec. 1; The Revised Statutes of the State of Indiana, 1843, Chap. 28, sec. 4; *Acts 1845/1846 (general),* Chap. 22, sec. 1., 35. Few declarations of intention existed in Indiana prior to 1818 with many occurring after this date. See also William Paterson, comp., *Laws of the State of New Jersey, 1703-1799,.* 123, 452 and Joseph Bloomfield, *Laws of the State of New Jersey, 1800-1811,* 172, Act of November 7, 1806. Kenneth Scott, "Resident Alien's Enabled to Hold Land in New York State, 1790-1825," *National Genealogical Society Quarterly* 67 (March 1979), 42-57, and Kenneth Scott and Rosame Coney, comp., *New York Alien Residents, 1825-1848* (Baltimore: Genealogical Publishing Co., 1978).

99. *Laws of the State of New York*, 1825, chapter 308; *Laws of the state of New York*, 1913, chapter 152. For additional information on how to use these unindexed ledgers and for an excellent study on the Archives' naturalization holdings, see "Naturalization & Related Records New York State Archives Information Leaflet #6," available at [www.sara.nysed.gov/holding/fact/natur-fahtm#intro].

100. Department of the Interior, *Report of the Commissioners of the General Land Office* (Washington: Government Printing Office, 1921), 63. For a discussion of homestead records see *Guide to Genealogical Research in the National Archives rev. ed. 1985* (Washington: National Archives and Records Service, 1982), 217. For a list of land offices in which homestead applications were filed, see National Archives, *Preliminary Inventory of the Land Entry Papers of the General Land Office*, No. 22, 1949. As to the current location of these records, see Kenneth Hawkins, comp., *Research in the Land Entry Files of the General Land Office*, (Washington: National Archives and Records Administration, 1997). A comprehensive study of land "case files" is found in William Dollarhide, "Forgotten Public Land Records: The Search for an Elusive File Folder," *Genealogy Bulletin* 43 (January/February 1998).

101. Revised, 1985. See pages 197-206, 246. For a discussion of the involvement of the Division of Naturalization with the U.S. Civil Service Commission and in implementing the steamboat-inspection laws, see *Reports of the Department of Commerce and Labor, 1908*, 291-92.

102. Act of March 2, 1907, 34 Stat. 1228, sec. 3; Act of September 22, 1922, 42 Stat. 1022, sec. 4; and Act of June 25, 1936, 49 Stat. 1917, sec. 1. U.S. Department of Labor, Immigration and Naturalization Service, *Rules and Regulations*, Rule 16, Subdivision B. 1936 Edition, effective December 1, 1936.

103. *Annual Report of the Attorney General of the United States*, 1941, (Washington: Government Printing Office, 1942), 237.

104. The records are a part of Record Group 85. For the New England states, the records are in NARA's Northeast Region (Boston), and those for New York City, 1792-1906, are in NARA's Northeastern Region, (New York City).

105. P. William Filby, ed. *Philadelphia Naturalization Records, 1791-1906* (Detroit: Gale Publishing, 1981).

106. The Nebraska Historical Society has a microfilm copy of the index to Nebraska and the western part of Iowa.

107. NARA's Southwest Region (Fort Worth) has a card index to naturalization, 1831-1906, for Louisiana and a bound index, 1853-1939, for Texas. NARA's Central Plains Region (Kansas City) has the index for Alabama and a single one for Nebraska and Western Iowa and for the eastern part of Iowa, parts of Wisconsin, Illinois and Indiana are at NARA's Regional Archives (Chicago). Full descriptions are available from the Internet at the Websites given in Appendix III. For a published list of NARA's Regional Archives holdings, see Loretto Dennis Szucs and Sandra Hargreaves Luebing, *The Archives A Guide to the National Archives Field Branches*, (Salt Lake City, UT: Ancestry Publishing, 1988), 172-176 and 250-26. Helpful is a set of maps showing what part of Iowa, Wisconsin, Illinois and Indiana are included. For descriptions of the indices see P. William Filby *Passenger and Immigration Lists Bibliography* (Detroit: Gale Research Co., 1981), #6401, #9280, and #9290-9314.

108. *An Index to Indiana Naturalization Records Found in Various Order Books of the Ninety Two Local Courts Prior to 1907* (Indianapolis: Indiana Historical Society, 1981).

109. *Reports of the Department of Labor, 1913,* 365.

110. *Halmgren v U.S.,* 217 U.S. 509 (1910).

111. *Printz v. U.S.,* 521 U.S.—, 138 L Ed 2d 914, 927. In addition, page 926 of the opinion observes: "The Government observes that statutes enacted by the first Congresses required state courts to record applications for citizenship . . . ." [This case determined the constitutionality of part of the "Brady Gun Bill."]

112. *State ex rel Board of Com'rs of Marion County v. Quill,* 102 N. E. 106.

113. Act of June 25, 1948, chapter 64, 5 62 Stat. 767(h).

114. See Immigration and Naturalization Service Manual M-154, Revised December 5, 1972. It is still a federal offense to reproduce naturalization records for unlawful authority. 18 U.S. C. 1426.

115. In 1985 Connecticut has joined other New England states in creating a regional repository of naturalization records at the NARA's Northeastern Region (Boston), by depositing Connecticut Superior Court naturalization records along with those under state court jurisdiction. The Connecticut state archives has a microfilm copy. See Connecticut State Library *Newsletter,* no.21, June, 1985, 8.

116. See, for example, Carleton E. Fisher, "Quality Assurance, "*National Genealogy Society Quarterly,* 53-4, 243-250. Mr. Fisher provides fifteen points, including "differentiate between accurate data and fact," "Compare data in official records with historical events," and "the name is not the thing." In addition, all genealogical research should be evaluated in accordance with Noel C. Stevenson, *Genealogical Evidence--A Guide to the Standard of Proof Relating to Pedigrees, Ancestry, Heirship and Family History* (Laguna Hills, CA: Aegean Park Press, 1989).

117. Christina K. Schaefer, *Guide to Naturalization Records of the United States,* (Baltimore: Genealogical Publishing Co., 1997), 105.

118. George Everton, Jr., The *Handy Book For Genealogists United States Of America,* eighth edition, (Logan, UT, Everton Publishers, Inc., 1991).

119. Charles Christopher Crittenden and Dan Lacy, ed., *The Historical Records of North Carolina,* (Raleigh: The North Carolina Historical Commission, 1938), volume 1, 97. Over 1200 naturalization papers in the North Carolina State Archives are abstracted in Betty J. Camin, *North Carolina Naturalizations, 1792-1860* (Mt. Airy, North Carolina, 1989).

120. For a fuller description of PERSI, see David Thackery, "Periodical Sources," *Ancestry* 12 (March/April 1994), 18-20.

121. For additional information on the USGenWeb Project, see *NGS/CIG Digest* (16-2) September October 1997 1 (part of the *NGS Newsletter* 23-5, September October 1997) and Jake Gehring, "The USGenWeb Project," *Ancestry* magazine, 15-4 (July/August 1997), 46.

122. See [www.localnet.com/~andrie/erie/erech.htm].

123. Write to the Immigration and Naturalization Service, 425 I Street, N.W., Washington, DC 20536, using form G-639, Application for a Search of the Records of the Immigration Naturalization

Service under FOIA. After April 1, 1956, write to the district office where the alien ancestor lived. Many major cities have an Immigration and Naturalization Service office which can assist you.

124. Stafford R. Cole, *Italian Genealogical Records*, (Salt Lake City, UT: Ancestry Publishing, 1995), 9; Sandra K. Ogle, "Genealogical Research in California," *National Genealogical Society Quarterly*, 76 (September 1988), 206. The LDS Family History Library Catalog shows many counties in that state having local court naturalization records into the 1950's.

125. Oscar *Handlin, Truth in History*, (Harvard University Press, 1979), 404-405.

126. Henry S. Dubester, *State Censuses An Annotated Bibliography Taken After the Year 1790 by States and Territories of the United States*, (New York: Burt Franklin, reprint 1949). This study gives data fields for each census and the sources, for further investigation. More recent is Ann S. Lainhart, *State Census Records*, (Baltimore: Genealogical Publishing Company, 1992).

 **Bibliographical Essay**

This essay is divided into three parts. The first discusses sources used in the research for this essay that might assist the reader in further investigation of the naturalization process. Next is a listing of general works on naturalization. Finally, there is a list of sources, incomplete, but representative, on where naturalization records or information about citizenship may be found. One can use this as a guide for location of information useful for individual research.

SOURCES ON NATURALIZATION

Primary research starts with the laws enacted by Congress, 1790-current, described as *United States Statutes at Large*. Major naturalization laws were enacted in 1790, 1795, 1798, 1802, 1824, 1906, 1918, 1929, 1940, 1952 and 1990. Many amending and supplemental acts also were passed. See notes for specific citations. A comprehensive study helpful to genealogists is *Laws Applicable to Immigration and Nationality*, Edition 1953, Immigration and Naturalization Service, Department of Justice (Washington: Government Printing Office, 1953), 1557 pages. Until a federal office was established in 1906, investigations by Congressional committees or executive departments provide basic information on nineteenth-century naturalization processes and problems. The most significant one was the *Report to the President of the Naturalization Commission,* House Document, 59th Congress, First Session, Document 45, which summarized earlier evaluations of naturalization irregularities in 1844, 1868, 1892-93, and 1903.

There are many general histories concerning American naturalization. Any of these can provide a framework for conceptualizing the processes and procedures, with such studies placed in an historical or sociological framework. Helpful is Bromwell, William J., *History of Immigration to the United States 1819-1885* (New York, New York: Augustus M. Kelly Reprint, 1969). It includes discussions regarding naturalization laws and petitions to Congress for liberalizing or tightening citizenship requirements. If an ancestor lived in an area where petitions originated, this book might lead one to a Congressional study. Recently, new general histories offering insight into naturalization issues have appeared. See, for example, Bredbenner, Candice Lewis. *A Nationality of Her Own: Women, Marriage, and the Law of Citizenship* (Berkeley: University of California Press, 1998). This study examines the 1907 law that removed American citizenship to native American women who married foreigners, and how women reacted to this politically.

For policy development and statistics, the annual reports of the federal agency exercising naturalization overview are essential. From 1906-1912 these are a part of the Department of Commerce and Labor; 1913-1940, a unit of the Department of Labor; and, since 1941, under the Department of Justice. The naturalization reports, 1942-1945, are in summary form only; and beginning in 1947 are issued as separate publications of the Immigration and Naturalization Service. In 1978 the Department of Justice began publishing its *Statistical Yearbook of the Immigration and Naturalization Service.* The 1979 *Yearbook* shows "Immigration by County for Decades 1820 -1979," table 13, 36-38. For statistical data, see U.S. Department of the Census, *Historical Statistics of the United States, Colonial Times to 1970*, Bicentennial edition, Part I, Chapter C. "International Migration and Naturalization," 97-120. (Washington: Government Printing Office, 1976). Valuable are: Table 89-119, "1820 - 1970 Immigration by Country," 105-109 and Table 168-180, which shows the number of women naturalized from 1923 through 1970. The *Statistical Abstract of the United States* first appeared in 1878. It may be easier to locate this rather than the various immigration and naturalization *Reports.* The 57th *Statistical Abstract of the United States, 1901*, for example, has "Number and Nationality of Immigrants Arrived in the United States From 1887 to 1901," Table 129, pages 416-417.

General overviews of naturalization exist. Helpful is a *Historical Sketch of Naturalization in the United States,* 1926, U.S. Department of Labor; and the second is a series of thirty-six lectures to the staff of the newly formed Immigration and Naturalization Service, 1934-1935. The following lectures are most helpful.

LECTURE	DATE	TITLE
4	3/05/1934	Legislative Background to the 1929 Registry Act
12	4/23/1934	Naturalization Procedure
13	4/30/1934	Records and Filing System
19	6/11/1934	Legal Research
25	12/03/1934	Documentary Evidence of Citizenship Status
34	2/04/1935	Derivative Citizenship

These lectures, cited fully in the notes, are distributed public documents and are found in many depository libraries.

Naturalization laws, rules, and regulations were published in a series of pamphlets beginning August 25, 1906. These are beneficial in studying the law and changes in rules affecting the information and format contained in naturalization records. Also useful are a series of *Directory of Courts Exercising Naturalization,* especially the 1963 directory. (The latter is available from the LDS Family History Library, roll 1730286.) Court histories and listings of naturalization records in WPA *Inventories of County Archives* also can be beneficial. One or more was published for forty-four states with none for Alaska, Connecticut, Hawaii, Maine, North Dakota, and Rhode Island. In addition 42 of the then existing 48 states published inventories of federal courts. The WPA published a separate *Guide to Naturalization Records in New Jersey,* 1941, which contains information on colonial naturalization laws. Also helpful are the statistical abstracts and manuscript census records, especially for 1830 and 1890-1930.

Most of the above are part of the public documents found in depository libraries throughout the United States. At least one regional depository is found in each state. They are designed for interlibrary loan under the Federal Depository policies and should be available wherever there is a library.

GENERAL PUBLICATIONS

Many states have genealogical guides available, both in book length and in articles. For the former, a list of genealogical books in print from the Library of Congress is available on the Internet through the Allen County Public Library web site. Between 1987 and 1994, the National Genealogical Society, in its *Quarterly*, published brief research guides to fifteen states and the District of Columbia (March, 1990); California (September, 1988); Colorado (June, 1989); Florida (June, 1988); Georgia (June, 1992); Indiana (June, 1991); Minnesota (March, 1989); Mississippi (March, 1988); Nebraska (December, 1989); North Carolina (March, 1987); Ohio (June, 1987); Oregon (March, 1991); South Carolina (December, 1987); Tennessee (June, 1993); Texas (September, 1987); and Virginia (September, 1994). These articles can identify sources, archives and institutions having information about people as well as more specific information, usually, about naturalization records.

Begin citizenship research by first attempting to locate biographical data on the immigrant ancestor in published county and city histories. Do not overlook the county atlases that were published from the 1870's - 1920's, a number of which contain "Patron Directories," giving name, age, place of birth, and year of arrival in the county. Many city and county directories are available on microfilm. Spear, Dorothea N., *Bibliography of American Directories Through 1860* (Worcester, MA: American Antiquarian Society, 1961), *City Directories of the United States, 1860-1901: Guide to the Microfilm Collection*, (Woodbridge, CT: Research Publications, 1983), and trade and professional directories can be found in Ethridge, James A. ed., *The Directory of Directories* (Detroit: Gale Research, 1980). Eicholtz, Alice, ed., Ancestry's *Redbook*, (revised 1992) gives a comprehensive list of state, county, and town sources and is valuable in determining the extent of records surviving on a county level. Everton, George, Jr., *The Handy Book for Genealogists*, 8th edition, 1991 not only contains similar information but also provides migration maps and listings of holdings of county level WPA Historical Records Survey county inventories.

There are two helpful sources for obtaining addresses and telephone numbers of clerks of courts. The first is updated annually each October: *Directory of State Court Clerks & County Courthouses*, (New York City: Want Publishing Company). There is a list of clerks of each court, an organizational chart of the current court structure in each state, and the available web site addresses. It also publishes a corresponding *Want's Federal-State Court Directory*, yearly. *The Sourcebook of County Court Records*, third edition, 1997, the Public Record Research Library, Tempe, Arizona, [www.brbpub.com] lists holdings as well as copy charges and methods of payment, current, as of date of publication.

From a wide variety of books and articles on use of naturalization records by genealogists, both in scope and depth, the following may be helpful. Neagles, James C., and Lila Lee Neagles, *Locating Your Immigrant Ancestor: A Guide to Naturalization Records* (Logan, UT: The Everton Publishers, revised 1986) combines narrative, charts, and illustrations for an overview of citizenship. More recent is Schaefer, Christina K., *Guide to Naturalization Records of the United States* (Baltimore, MD: Genealogical Publishing Co., 1997). Loretto Dennis Szucs and Sandra Hargreaves Luebing, editors, *The Source: A Guide-*

book of American Genealogy (Salt Lake City: Ancestry Publishing Company, revised 1997) contains a comprehensive chapter on "Finding Immigrant Origins," by Kory L. Meyerink and Loretto Dennis Szucs, Chapter 13, 441-520. Pages 472-520 relate directly to naturalization records. The chapter has an extensive bibliography. Szucs and Luebing also have published *The Archives, A guide to the Nation Archives Field Branches* (Salt Lake City: Ancestry, 1988). It provides in print as of date of publication what is now available in *The Guide to Federal Records in the National Archives of the United States*, 3 volumes, (1996), which is available on the Internet, as well as NARA's Regional Archival holdings. Consult listings for Record Groups 21, 85 and 200. Also helpful is Schwartz, Gregory C., "From Whence They Came: Locating an Immigrant's Origin Through Naturalization Records," *The Genealogical Helper* 34-6 (November-December, 1980): 11-15. Dalby, Barbara M., "Naturalization Record: Minors in the U.S. District Court for the Southern District of Illinois," *Illinois State Genealogical Society Quarterly, V1-1* (Spring 1974), 36, discusses the legal ramifications of copying. These citations represent a few of many on the subject. Each in its own way, as does this book, adds to the general knowledge of naturalization for a better understanding by genealogists. More work is required, including further research in frauds and private bills for naturalization presented before Congress.

SOURCES OF RECORDS

For the following, and other references, read each introduction. Several minutes reading can give one the scope of the publication and can save one from wasted time and embarrassing inquiries.

Most of these publications have been done by genealogists for genealogists. Look equally to those written by record custodians, as archivists and librarians, who not only field genealogical questions but study records in the context of their creation. They know the genealogy of the record. Some authors can be misinformed about the records they describe and can be inaccurate, incomplete, or misleading. It may be advisable to consult several sources for each fact or record sought and to contact record custodians for the current status and location of naturalization records.

Concerning lists of naturalization records, these major sources exist. The first is Filby, P. William, editor, *Passenger and Immigration Lists Bibliography 1538-1900* (Detroit: Gale Research Co., 1981). Check the index under "naturalization" and also under each state. While many states are under "naturalization," Louisiana is not. It has its own subheading of "naturalization." In 1984 the *First Supplement* appeared under the same title, editor, and publisher. It contains a combined index which is superior to the first volume. Consult also the listings of various microfilmed naturalization court records housed at the LDS Family History Library, Salt Lake City. In addition to checking national, state, or county localities for "naturalization," check the catalog for court minute books that have been filmed, including those for probate courts.

A second major class of publications are inventory records from institutions holding records, whether names are published or not. Of significance here are the lists of the National Archives and the regional Federal Archives and of the various states. *The Guide to Federal Records in the National Archives of the United States*, 3 volumes, (1996), is the single best source for federal government holdings, not only on Naturalization records, but on courts, passport applications, homestead applications, and special classes of employment which required citizenship.

To pinpoint what records were created in state and local courts, two sources are helpful. The first is the listing of materials of the Historical Records Survey, WPA *Bibliography of Research Projects Reports, Check List of Historical Records Survey Publication,* Technical Series, Research and Resources Bibliography 7 (Washington: WPA, 1943), reprinted by the Genealogical Publishing Co., Baltimore, 1969. This publication lists the inventories generated on the county level for 44 states as of the 1940 era. Even if one does not exist for the county in which you are especially interested, for that state any one inventory will familiarize you with the local court structure and names. The second is the use of PERSI, which can lead one to articles about or from naturalization records. Some naturalization materials continue to be discovered since publication of these WPA inventories. [See *Illinois State Genealogical Quarterly,* XVII-1 (Spring, 1985); 1, for naturalization records recently discovered in Ogle County, Illinois.] Some updates of the inventory have been published. See, for example, "An Inventory of Jefferson County Records," Samuel W. Thomas, *The Filson Club Quarterly:* 44-4 (October, 1970): 321-55. This listing shows the diversity of courts for Jefferson County, Kentucky (Louisville). Finally, use the Internet.

Published and on-line works provide descriptive and locator information both about ancestors and about the records themselves. One can save much research time and show knowledge to a court clerk that may assist that person in locating the record sought.